'This is dedicated to the one I love.'
The Mamas & The Papas (1967)

1000 GREAT QUOTATIONS

FOR BUSINESS, MANAGEMENT & TRAINING

DAVID WILLIAMS

an
encouraging excellence
publication

GNP

Published by
GNP Ltd
10 Market Place
Hexham
Northumberland
NE46 1XG
England

ISBN 0 9531 5101 8

Printed in Great Britain by NB Group

ABOUT THE AUTHOR

David Williams runs his own management development company GNP, based in the North of England. He acts as a consultant and trainer for a wide range of public and private sector organisations, and is behind some of Britain's largest management conferences and seminars. He is the creator of the **Encouraging Excellence** programme, promoting innovative management thinking and best practice through inspiring events and productive networks. David is married to the co-founder of GNP, Paula Williams, and they have three stimulating children.

INTRODUCTION

I compiled this collection because I needed it myself. That is to say my mountain of notes, cuttings and print-outs was threatening a landslide in my store cupboard. I could lay a hand on an appropriate quotation just when I required it, provided I had two days' notice of the occasion and nothing else to do but sift through the pile built up over several years.

This project has put a semblance of order back into my life and on the way has provided me with a great deal of pleasure as I rediscovered some of the wise and witty observations that stirred me enough to write them down at the time, only to bury them under my own disorder.

Indeed one of the most difficult tasks in selecting material for the book has been deciding what to leave out. It is a highly subjective choice, one which is bound to reveal my own slants and prejudices. I have tried, however, to keep the reader constantly in mind. I hope you will find among these thousand odd quotations many that apply to your experience in the world of business, management or training, even though many stem from seemingly unrelated disciplines such as sport or mass entertainment, and may have been originally spoken or written in an age quite different from the one we know today.

Although I have tried to ensure as much variety as possible and offer a wide range of authors, some names do crop up again and again. The American essayist, Ralph Waldo Emerson, for example, is a notable quotable. Ironically he is the man who once famously said: 'I hate quotations.'

The astonishing scientist Albert Einstein is another I keep returning to, especially for his comments on creativity and learning. Motor manufacturer Henry Ford was a master of the memorable aphorism, as was author Mark Twain.

I have tried to reflect modern management thinking with an assortment of observations from contemporary 'gurus', especially those I most admire and in some cases have worked with - Tom Peters, Rosabeth Moss Kanter, Warren Bennis, Peter Drucker. I do hope that the tiny nuggets of business philosophy I have scattered among these pages will inspire you to discover or renew acquaintance with their stimulating books or attend one of their electrifying presentations.

Not everyone represented here is well known. Biographical detail on the less than famous has been difficult to come by, which is why some dates are missing. In a few cases I have not even been able to say with certainty what they do or did for a living, but I have been reluctant to lose some of my favourite quotations for want of a little information. Not that I would go so far as author Anatole France who wrote:

'When a thing has been said and well said, have no scruple; take it and copy it. Give references? Why should you? Either your readers know where you have taken the passage and the precaution is needless, or they do not know and you humiliate them.'

One of the difficulties that causes the scrupulous researcher is pinning down a quotation definitively to an original source. Some of the greatest orators (President John F Kennedy for one) thought nothing of slightly altering another's observation or simply importing it wholesale into their own 'original' speeches and writings. Others may have done it unconsciously.

For the most part I have looked for the oldest attribution I could find, but there are bound to be errors and accidental distortions. This book makes no pretence to be a scholarly work, but I have tried to be as accurate as this elusive subject allows.

Any reader who can help fill the gaps or correct mistakes is invited to contact me and I will provide due acknowledgement in a future edition.

As a British writer one thing that struck me forcibly while I was researching attributions was how many of these quotations come from American mouths and pens. This is not entirely explained by the sheer size of the country or its position as the world's most powerful nation. There is something cultural at work here too.

My contention is that Americans learned the value of the 'soundbite' long before the advent of mass media. The relentless presence of TV images across US society today may have developed their habit of packaging speech in exploding parcels, but the tendency seems indigenous.

Even a casual comparison of US and English language patterns up to 200 years ago shows the Americans to be far less inclined to the elaborate verbal courtesies and locutions that characterised English opinion-formers of a past age. Vestiges of that linguistic difference (steeped, as it is, in class, education and tradition) persist today, though they are gradually being eroded by the forces of globalisation.

I have wreaked my revenge on this horde of quotable Americans by ruthlessly anglicising their spelling. The Empire strikes back. As the critic James Agate wrote:

'Your Englishman, confronted by something abnormal, will always pretend that it isn't there. If, however, you force him to look into it, he'll at once pretend that he sees the object not for what it is but for something that he would like it to be.'

Note Agate's employment of the masculine collective pronoun, as they used to call it in my grammar school days. Political correctness has booted such usage out of contemporary speech (and robbed it of a certain elegance), but you will find the older quotations in this book dominated by 'he' and 'man'. Please blame history not this author and adjust for gender.

I have sorted this selection of quotations alphabetically into themes and subjects that I trust readers will find appropriate. Some of the distinctions are quite subtle; there are obvious links between Achievement, Success and Winning for example, and between Failure and Mistakes. I recommend 'surfing' around associated themes for the best results. I toyed for a while with creating a comprehensive index of authors and terms, but eventually resisted it for the simple reason that this is the sort of book that rewards browsing.

I hope I have succeeded in avoiding the predictable and over-familiar. I want you to be surprised by unexpected gems, to experience the same pleasure I felt when I first came across them, to nod your head at succinct sagacity, smile at truths eloquently revealed, have your mind expanded by insightful observation and your heart lifted by inspirational thoughts.

I have tried to sow a little wit among the wisdom - a seedling from Groucho Marx here, from Woody Allen there. Every so often a cartoon character I have uninventively named Murphy pops up with one of those ironic maxims that send up business and office life and help us remember what my friend Benjamin Zander calls Rule Number 6: 'Don't take yourself so goddam' seriously.'

Thanks to cartoonist Frank Taylor for creating the Murphy character and to his colleagues at NB Group for bringing the book to print. Working backwards along the production line, thanks to Julie Porter and Sue Little for converting my bits of paper into a workable manuscript, to Laura James and my son Joe for their hours of help researching sources, and especially to my wife Paula, not only for encouraging me to start the project but for shaping it into a publishable form.

I like to feel the reader is part of the team too and welcome constructive comment, help and advice for a future edition of this book. Please e-mail me: david@gnp.co.uk.

DAVID WILLIAMS

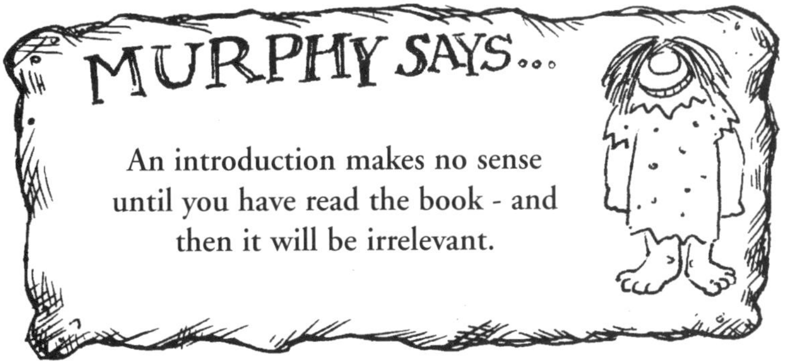

ABILITY

Whether you believe you can, or whether you believe you can't, you're absolutely right.

Henry Ford, US automobile manufacturer, engineer (1863-1947)

Every man has one thing he can do better than anyone else - and usually it's reading his own handwriting.

G Norman Collie, Scottish mountaineer

If a man is called to be a streetsweeper, he should sweep streets even as Michelangelo painted, or Beethoven played music, or Shakespeare wrote poetry. He should sweep streets so well that all the hosts of heaven and earth will pause to say, here lived a great streetsweeper who did his job well.

Martin Luther King Jr, US civil rights leader (1929-1968)

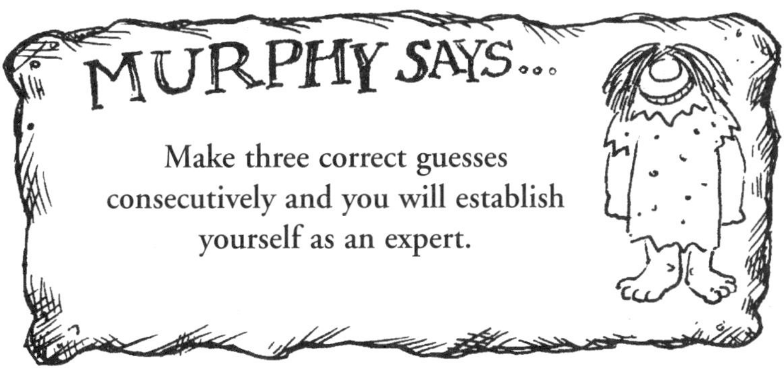

A human being should be able to change a diaper, plan an invasion, butcher a hog, conn a ship, design a building, write a sonnet, balance accounts, build a wall, set a bone, comfort the dying, take orders, give orders, cooperate, act alone, solve equations, analyse a new problem, pitch manure, programme a computer, cook a tasty meal, fight efficiently, die gallantly. Specialisation is for insects.

Lazarus Long, character in a novel by Robert Heinlein (1907-1988)

Talent never asks, 'Will they like it?' Talent pleases itself. That's the difference between talent and ordinary.

Larry King, US talk show host (b. 1933)

People's beliefs about their abilities have a profound effect on those abilities. Ability is not a fixed property; there is a huge variability in how you perform. People who have a sense of self-efficacy bounce back from failure; they approach things in terms of how to handle them rather than worrying about what can go wrong.

Albert Bandura, US psychologist (b. 1925)

ACHIEVEMENT

Lord, grant that I may always desire more than I can accomplish.

Michelangelo, Italian sculptor, painter, architect, poet (1475-1564)

Destiny is not a matter of chance, it is a matter of choice; it is not a thing to be waited for, it is a thing to be achieved.

William Jennings Bryan, US statesman (1860-1925)

You cannot do anything better in this life than run your own perfect race.

Roger Black, British athlete (b. 1966)

The moment of victory is much too short to live for that and nothing else.

Martina Navratilova, Czech-born US tennis player (b. 1956)

The greatest pleasure in life is doing what people say you cannot do.

Walter Bagehot, British author, economist (1826-1877)

Most of the things worth doing in the world have been declared impossible before they were done.

Louis Brandeis, US supreme court justice (1856-1941)

It is not the mountain we conquer but ourselves.

Sir Edmund Hillary, New Zealand mountaineer and explorer (b. 1919)

In Italy for thirty years under the Borgias they had warfare, terror, murder and bloodshed, but they produced Michelangelo, Leonardo da Vinci and the Renaissance. In Switzerland they had brotherly love, they had five hundred years of democracy and peace, and what did they produce? The cuckoo clock.

Harry Lime, character in 'The Third Man' by Graham Greene (1904-1991)

When love and skill work together, expect a masterpiece.

John Ruskin, British writer, art critic (1819-1900)

Too low they build who build beneath the stars.

Edward Young, British poet, dramatist, literary critic (1683-1765)

We judge ourselves by what we are capable of doing; others judge us by what we have done.

Henry Wadsworth Longfellow, US poet (1807-1882)

Some of the world's greatest feats were accomplished by people not smart enough to know they were impossible.

Doug Larson, US marketeer, writer

ACTION

You can't leave footprints in the sands of time if you're sitting on your butt. And who wants to leave buttprints in the sands of time?

Bob Moawald

People are always blaming their circumstances for what they are. I don't believe in circumstances. The people who get on in the world are the people who get up and look for the circumstances they want and if they can't find them, make them.

George Bernard Shaw, Irish playwright, essayist (1856-1950)

I never worry about action, but only about inaction.

Winston Churchill, British Prime Minister (1874-1965)

If there is no wind, row.

Twenty years from now you will be more disappointed by the things you didn't do than by the ones you did do. So throw off the bowlines. Sail away from the safe harbour. Catch the trade winds in your sails. Explore. Dream. Discover.

Mark Twain, US author (1835-1910)

If your ship doesn't come in, swim out to it.

Jonathan Winters, US actor (b. 1925)

It is not enough to have knowledge, one must also apply it. It is not enough to have wishes, one must also accomplish.

Johann Wolfgang von Goethe, German poet, letter-writer (1749-1832)

The great end of life is not knowledge but action.

T H Huxley, British biologist, philosopher (1825-1895)

We have to understand that the world can only be grasped by action, not by contemplation. The hand is more important than the eye. The hand is the cutting edge of the mind.

Jacob Bronowski, British mathematician, scientist (1908-1974)

You can't build a reputation on what you are going to do.

Henry Ford, US automobile manufacturer, engineer (1863-1947)

Life doesn't give you all the practice races you need.

Jesse Owens, US athlete (1913-1980)

It is better to light a candle than to curse the darkness.

Confucius, Chinese philosopher, teacher (551-479 BC)

Life is a great big canvas - throw all the paint on it you can.

Danny Kaye, US comedian, actor (1913-1987)

Ten people who speak make more noise than ten thousand who are silent.

Napoleon Bonaparte, French soldier, statesman, revolutionary (1769-1821)

Well done is better than well said.

Benjamin Franklin, US statesman, author, scientist (1706-1790)

It is time for all of us to stand and cheer for the doer, the achiever - the one who recognises the challenges and does something about it.

Vince Lombardi, US football coach (1913-1970)

As I grow older, I pay less attention to what men say. I just watch what they do.

Andrew Carnegie, Scottish industrialist, philanthropist (1835-1919)

If you're in the penalty area and don't know what to do with the ball, put it in the net and we'll discuss the options later.

Bob Paisley, British football manager (1919-1996)

You miss 100% of the shots you don't take.

Wayne Gretzky, Canadian ice hockey champion (b. 1961)

I have found the best way to give advice to your children is to find out what they want and then advise them to do it.

Harry S Truman, US President (1884-1972)

It is not the critic who counts; not the man who points out how the strong man stumbled or where the doer of deeds could have done them better. The credit belongs to the man who is actually in the arena; whose face is marred by dust and sweat and blood; who strives valiantly; who errs and comes short again and again; who knows the great enthusiasms, the great devotions, and spends himself in a worthy cause; who, at the best, knows the triumph of high achievement; and who, at the worst, if he fails, at least fails while daring greatly, so that his place shall never be with those cold and timid souls who knew neither victory nor defeat.

Theodore Roosevelt, US President (1858-1919)

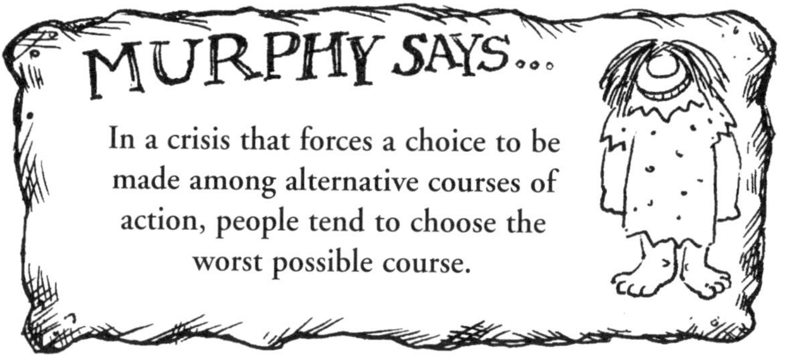

There are really only three types of people: those who make things happen, those who watch things happen, and those who say, 'What happened?'.

Ann Landers, US advice columnist (b. 1918)

Conditions are never just right. People who delay action until all factors are favourable do nothing.

William Feather, US author, publisher (1889-1981)

Be like a duck. Calm on the surface, but always paddling like the dickens underneath.

Michael Caine, British actor (b. 1922)

Dream as if you'll live forever. Live as if you'll die today.

James Dean, US actor (1931-1955)

ADVERTISING

Advertising is of the very essence of democracy. An election goes on every minute of the business day across the counters of hundreds of thousands of stores and shops where the customers state their preferences and determine which manufacturer and which product shall be the leader today, and which shall lead tomorrow.

Bruce Barton, US author, advertising executive (1886-1967)

If you make a product good enough the public will make a path to your door, says the philosopher. But if you want the public in sufficient numbers, you would better construct a highway. Advertising is that highway.

William Randolph Hearst, US newspaper magnate (1863-1951)

Many a small thing has been made large by the right kind of advertising.

Mark Twain, US author (1835-1910)

Promise, large promise, is the soul of an advertisement.

Samuel Johnson, British poet, critic, lexicographer (1709-1784)

In our factory, we make lipstick. In our advertising, we sell hope.

Charles Revlon, US businessman (1906-1975)

The philosophy behind much advertising is based on the old observation that every man is really two men - the man he is and the man he wants to be.

William Feather, US author, publisher (1889-1981)

Great designers seldom make great advertising men, because they get overcome by the beauty of the picture - and forget that merchandise must be sold.

James Randolph Adams, US advertising executive

When you advertise fire-extinguishers, open with the fire.

David Ogilvy, US advertising executive, author (b. 1911)

It is not the purpose of the ad or commercial to make the reader or listener say 'My, what a clever ad.' It is the purpose of advertising to make the reader or listener say, 'I believe I'll buy one when I'm shopping tomorrow.'

Morris Hite, US advertising guru, author

We want consumers to say, 'That's a hell of a product' instead of, 'That's a hell of an ad.'

Leo Burnett, US advertising executive (1891-1971)

The product that will not sell without advertising will not sell profitably with advertising.

Albert Lasker, US businessman, father of modern advertising (1880-1952)

Doing business without advertising is like winking at a girl in the dark. You know what you are doing but nobody else does.

Edgar Watson Howe, US editor, author, essayist (1853-1937)

The business that considers itself immune to the necessity for advertising sooner or later finds itself immune to business.

Derby Brown

Let advertisers spend the same amount of money improving their product that they do on advertising and they wouldn't have to advertise it.

Will Rogers, US actor, humorist (1879-1935)

The best ad is a good product.

Alan H Meyer, US academic, business author

The secret of all effective originality in advertising is not the creation of new and tricky words and pictures, but one of putting familiar words and pictures into new relationships.

Leo Burnett, US advertising executive (1891-1971)

The trouble with us in America isn't that the poetry of life has turned into prose, but that it has turned into advertising copy.

Louis Kronenberger, US critic (1904-1980)

The art of advertisement, after the American manner, has introduced into all our lives such a lavish use of superlatives, that no standard of value whatever is intact.

Wyndham Lewis, British author, painter (1882-1957)

Advertising in the final analysis should be news. If it is not news it is worthless.

Adolph S Ochs, US newspaper publisher (1858-1935)

Asked about the power of advertising in research surveys, most agree that it works, but not on them.

Eric Clark, US advertising guru, author

I know half the money I spend on advertising is wasted, but I can never find out which half.

John Wanamaker, US merchant, retail executive (1838-1922)

The value of an advertisement is in inverse ratio to the number of times it has been used.

Raymond Rubicam, US advertising executive (1892-1978)

AGE

What a distressing contrast there is between the radiant intelligence of the child and the feeble mentality of the average adult.

Sigmund Freud, Austrian founder of psychoanalysis (1856-1939)

A child of five would understand this. Send somebody to fetch a child of five.

Groucho Marx, US comic actor (1890-1977)

Strategies are okayed in boardrooms that even a child would say are bound to fail. The problem is, there is never a child in the boardroom.

Victor Palmieri, US executive, lawyer (b. 1930)

Every child is an artist. The problem is how to remain an artist once he grows up.

Pablo Picasso, Spanish painter (1881-1973)

No matter how old you get, if you can keep the desire to be creative, you're keeping the man-child alive.

John Cassavetes, US actor, director (1929-1989)

The young do not know enough to be prudent, and therefore they attempt the impossible, and achieve it, generation after generation.

Pearl S Buck, US author (1892-1973)

I'm not young enough to know everything.

J M Barrie, British dramatist, author (1860-1937)

The ageing process has you firmly in its grasp if you never get the urge to throw a snowball.

Doug Larson, US marketeer, writer

Anyone who stops learning is old, whether at twenty or eighty. Anyone who keeps learning stays young. The greatest thing in life is to keep your mind young.

Henry Ford, US automobile manufacturer, engineer (1863-1947)

The man who views the world at 50 the same as he did at 20 has wasted 30 years of his life.

Muhammad Ali, US heavyweight boxing champion (b.1942)

Nothing is more dishonourable than an old man, heavy with years, who has no other evidence of his having lived long except his age.

Seneca, Roman philosopher, statesman, author (3 BC-65 AD)

There is a fountain of youth: it is your mind, your talents, the creativity you bring to your life and the lives of the people you love. When you learn to tap this source, you will have truly defeated age.

Sophia Loren, Italian actress (b. 1934)

ATTITUDE

The greatest discovery of any generation is that a human being can alter his life by altering his attitude.

William James, US philosopher, psychologist (1842-1910)

There are no menial jobs, only menial attitudes.

William Bennett, US federal official (b. 1943)

The optimist sees the rose and not its thorns; the pessimist stares at the thorns, oblivious to the rose.

Kahlil Gibran, Lebanese philosopher, author, poet (1883-1931)

Science may have found a cure for most evils; but it has found no remedy for the worst of them all - the apathy of human beings.

Helen Keller, US writer, lecturer (1880-1968)

Students with high hopes set themselves higher goals and know how to work hard to attain them. When you compare students of equivalent intellectual aptitude on their academic achievements, what sets them apart is hope.

C R Snyder, US sociologist (b. 1924)

There is no bottom to worse.

People who are optimistic see a failure due to something that can be changed so that they can succeed next time around, while pessimists take the blame for failure, ascribing it to some lasting characteristic they are helpless to change.

Daniel Goleman, US psychologist, author (b.1946)

Men are disturbed not by things, but by the view which they take of them.

Epictetus (1st century BC)

The art of being yourself at your best is the art of unfolding your personality into the person you want to be. Be gentle with yourself, learn to love yourself, to forgive yourself, for only as we have the right attitude toward ourselves can we have the right attitude toward others.

Wilfred Peterson, US poet, moralist

BEGINNINGS

If we wait for the moment when everything, absolutely everything is ready, we shall never begin.

Ivan Turgenev, Russian author (1818-1883)

A man would do nothing if he waited until he could do it so well that no one could find fault.

John Henry Newman, British religious leader, prelate, author (1801-1890)

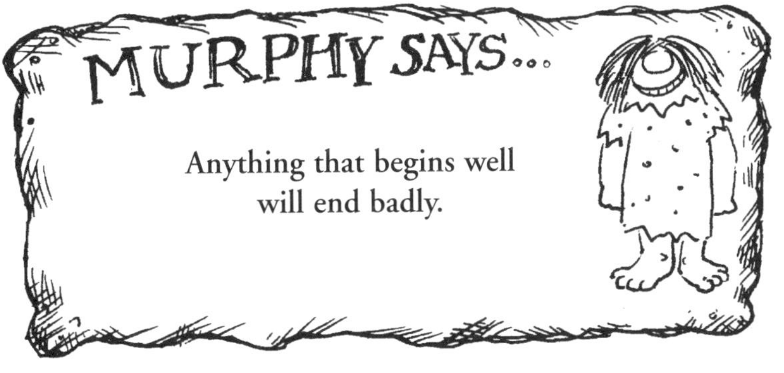

What you can do, or dream you can, begin it; boldness has genius, power and magic in it.

Johann Wolfgang von Goethe, German poet, letter-writer (1749-1832)

How wonderful it is that nobody need wait a single moment before starting to improve the world.

Anne Frank, German Jewish diarist, concentration camp victim (1929-1945)

Let him that would move the world, first move himself.

Socrates, Greek philosopher (469-399 BC)

He has half the deed done who has made a beginning.

Horace, Roman poet (65-8 BC)

The way to get started is to quit talking and start doing.

Walt Disney, US artist, film producer (1901-1966)

The creation of a thousand forests is in one acorn.

Ralph Waldo Emerson, American essayist, poet (1803-1882)

BREVITY

Brevity is a great charm of eloquence.

Marcus Tullius Cicero, Roman statesman, orator (106-43 BC)

The most valuable of all talents is that of never using two words when one will do.

Thomas Jefferson, US President (1741-1826)

Beware of the fool whose volume of words is as that of ten men, a hundred arrows shot and each one wide of the target. If thou art wise, shoot one and that one straight.

Sadi, Iranian Poet (1184-12??)

It is my ambition to say in ten sentences what others say in a whole book.

Friedrich Nietzsche, German philosopher, poet (1844-1900)

A specification that will not fit on one page of 8.5 x 11 inch paper cannot be understood.

Mark Ardis, US software engineer

It is more interesting to explore a topic than to exhaust it.

Mark McCormack, US sports agent (b. 1930)

If you can't say it in 30 seconds, you probably can't say it at all. If you know, you can make any point very well in 30 seconds.

Terry Mayo, US TV news presenter

BUREAUCRACY

Every revolution evaporates and leaves behind only the slime of a new bureaucracy.

Franz Kafka, Czechoslovakian author (1883-1924)

The only thing that saves us from bureaucracy is its inefficiency.

Eugene McCarthy, US author, senator (b. 1916)

Bureaucrats write memoranda both because they appear to be busy when they are writing and because the memos, once written, immediately become proof that they were busy.

Charles Peters, US editor, author (b. 1926)

The government is extremely fond of amassing great quantities of statistics. These are raised to the nth degree, the cube roots are extracted, and the results are arranged into elaborate and impressive displays. What must be kept ever in mind, however, is that in every case, the figures are first put down by a village watchman, and he puts down anything he damn well pleases.

Sir Josiah Stamp, British economist, businessman (1880-19??)

Useless laws weaken the necessary laws.

Charles de Secondat Montesquieu, French philosopher, jurist (1689-1755)

CHANGE

The one unchangeable certainty is that nothing is unchangeable or certain.

John F Kennedy, US President (1917-1963)

To live is to change, and to be perfect is to have changed often.

John Henry Newman, British religious leader, prelate, author (1801-1890)

You cannot become what you want to be by remaining what you are.

Max De Pree, US business executive, management author

Everyone thinks of changing the world, but no one thinks of changing himself.

Leo Tolstoy, Russian author (1828-1910)

God prevent we should ever be twenty years without a revolution.

Thomas Jefferson, US President (1741-1826)

It is not the strongest of the species that survive nor the most intelligent, but the ones most responsive to change.

Charles Darwin, British naturalist (1809-1882)

The world hates change, yet it is the only thing that has brought progress.

Charles Kettering, US engineer, inventor (1876-1958)

In life, change is inevitable. In business, change is vital.

Warren Bennis, US academic, management author (b. 1925)

When you're through changing, you're through.

Bruce Barton, US author, advertising executive (1886-1967)

If in the last few years you haven't discarded a major opinion or acquired a new one, check your pulse. You may be dead.

Frank Gelett Burgess, US humorist, illustrator (1866-1951)

When the wind blows some people build walls, others build windmills.

Peter Hawkins, US psychologist

Every organisation has to prepare for the abandonment of everything it does.

Peter Drucker, US management author, consultant (b. 1909)

When the rate of change outside is greater than the rate of change inside the end is in sight.

Jack Welch, US executive, utility chief (b. 1935)

Faced with the choice between changing one's mind and proving that there is no need to do so, almost everybody gets busy on the proof.

William Bridges, US engineer, researcher, educator (b. 1934)

Change is not merely necessary to life - it is life.

Alvin Toffler, US management author, editor (b. 1928)

The art of progress is to preserve order amid change and to preserve change amid order.

Alfred North Whitehead, British philosopher, mathematician (1861-1947)

Organisations change in units of one.

Peter Sole, British IT researcher

CHANGE AGENTS

The only thing necessary for evil to triumph is that good people do nothing - you must be the change that you want to see in the world.

Mahatma Gandhi, Indian nationalist leader (1869-1948)

There is nothing more difficult to carry out, nor more doubtful of success, nor more dangerous to handle, than to institute a new order of things.

Niccolo Machiavelli, Italian political theorist (1469-1527)

Think of yourselves as pioneers of a new age - you are not merely discovering a new world, you are helping to shape it.

David Williams, British management author, presenter (b. 1950)

Don't be afraid to take a big step if one is indicated. You can't cross a chasm in two small jumps.

David Lloyd George, British Prime Minister (1863-1945)

Any change or reform you make is going to have consequences you don't like.

Another contributory factor to failure is that many top managers are now so removed from their underlings that they wildly underestimate how long it takes to embed really fundamental change. All too often impatient managers signal a new direction even before those at the bottom have executed the last one. Not surprisingly, the result of such inconsistencies is change indigestion.

Simon Caulkin, British journalist

Become a student of change. It is the only thing that will remain constant.

Anthony J D'Angelo, US educationist, author

When I was a young man, I wanted to change the world. I found it was difficult to change the world, so I tried to change my nation. When I found I couldn't change the nation, I began to focus on my town. I couldn't change the town and, as an older man, I tried to change my family. Now as an old man, I realise the only thing I can change is myself, and suddenly I realise that if long ago I had changed myself, I could have made an impact on my family. My family and I could have made an impact on our town. Their impact could have changed the nation and I could indeed have changed the world.

Unknown monk (1100 AD)

COLLABORATION

If you have come here to do something for me, you are wasting your time; if you have come here because your transformation is directly involved with mine, let's get to work.

Australian Aborigine leader to a social worker

In the long history of humankind (and animalkind too) those who learned to collaborate and improvise most effectively have prevailed.

Charles Darwin, British naturalist (1809-1882)

None of us is as smart as all of us.

Chinese proverb

I not only use all the brains I have, but all I can borrow.

Woodrow Wilson, US President (1856-1924)

If you have an apple and I have an apple and we exchange these apples then you and I will still each have one apple. But if you have an idea and I have an idea and we exchange these ideas, then each of us will have two ideas.

George Bernard Shaw, Irish playwright, essayist (1856-1950)

Many ideas grow better when transplanted into another mind than in the one where they sprang up.

Oliver Wendell Holmes, US essayist, poet (1809-1894)

Great discoveries and improvements invariably involve the cooperation of many minds.

Alexander Graham Bell, Scottish inventor (1847-1922)

We are all angels with only one wing; we can only fly while embracing each other.

Luciano de Crescenzo, Italian author (b. 1928)

Every man works better when he has companions working in the same line, and yielding to the stimulus of suggestion, comparison, emulation. Great things have of course been done by solitary workers; but they have usually been done with double the pains they would have cost if they had been produced in more genial circumstances.

Henry James, US author (1843-1916)

COMMITMENT

Change does not take time - it takes commitment.

Thomas Crum, US management consultant, presenter

Nothing great will ever be achieved without great men, and men are great only if they are determined to be so.

Charles de Gaulle, French President, general (1890-1970)

Never doubt that a small group of thoughtful, committed citizens can change the world; indeed it's the only thing that ever does.

Margaret Mead, US anthropologist (1901-1978)

Commit yourself to a dream. Nobody who tries to do something great but fails is a total failure. Why? Because he can always rest assured that he succeeded in life's most important battle - he defeated his fear of trying.

Robert Schuller, US clergyman, author (b. 1926)

Consider the postage stamp. Its usefulness consists in the ability to stick to one thing till it gets there.

Josh Billings, US humorist (1818-1885)

Individual commitment to a group effort - that is what makes a team work, a company work, a society work, a civilisation work.

Vince Lombardi, US football coach (1913-1970)

Everything's in the mind. That's where it all starts. Knowing what you want is the first step towards getting it.

Mae West, US actress (1893-1980)

Faithless is he that says farewell when the road darkens.

Gimli, character in a novel by J R R Tolkien (1892-1973)

COMMUNICATION

I know that you believe that you understood what you think I said, but I am not sure you realise that what you heard is not what I meant.

Robert McCloskey, US diplomat (b. 1922)

The single biggest problem in communication is the illusion that it has taken place.

George Bernard Shaw, Irish playwright, essayist (1856-1950)

Inform all the troops that communications have completely broken down.

Ashleigh Brilliant, British philosopher, author (b. 1933)

A leader cannot afford to be a good communicator. He must be a great communicator.

William Hodges, US Federal judge (b. 1934)

If an organisation is to work effectively, the communication should be through the most effective channel regardless of the organisation chart.

David Packard, US electrical engineer, entrepeneur (1912-1996)

If you don't give people information, they'll make up something to fill the void.

Carla O'Dell, US management consultant, author

I used to think I was poor. Then they told me I wasn't poor, I was needy. Then they told me it was self-defeating to think of myself as needy. I was deprived. (Oh not deprived but rather underprivileged.) Then they told me that underprivileged was overused. I was disadvantaged. I still don't have a dime. But I have a great vocabulary.

Jules Feiffer, US cartoonist, author (b. 1929)

It often shows an excellent command of language to say nothing.

Karol Newlin

COMPETITION

Every morning in Africa, a gazelle wakes up. It knows it must outrun the fastest lion or it will be killed. Every morning in Africa, a lion wakes up. It knows it must run faster than the slowest gazelle, or it will starve. It doesn't matter whether you're a lion or a gazelle - when the sun comes up, you'd better be running.

African proverb

To conquer the enemy without resorting to war is the most desirable. The highest form of generalship is to conquer the enemy by strategy.

Sun Tzu, Chinese military strategist, general (4th century BC)

The biggest things are always the easiest to do because there is no competition.

Sir William C Van Horne, Canadian railway magnate

Competition brings out the best in products, and the worst in people.

David Sarnoff, US researcher

Do your work with your whole heart, and you will succeed - there's so little competition.

Elbert Hubbard, US publisher, editor (1856-1915)

COMPUTERS

The computer business is changing so quickly these days that sometimes we feel as if we're in the fresh-produce business.

Safi Quereshy, US executive, AST research

Computers are useless. They can only give you answers.

Pablo Picasso, Spanish painter (1881-1973)

No computer has ever been designed that is ever aware of what it's doing; but most of the time, we aren't either.

Marvin Minsky, US author (b. 1927)

The real danger is not that computers will begin to think like men, but that men will begin to think like computers.

Sydney Harris, US judge (b. 1917)

The computer can't tell you the emotional story. It can give you the exact mathematical design, but what's missing is the eyebrows.

Frank Zappa, US musician (1940-1993)

If you put tomfoolery into a computer, nothing comes out but tomfoolery. But this tomfoolery, having passed through a very expensive machine, is somehow ennobled and no-one dares criticise it.

Pierre Gallois

Software suppliers are trying to make their software packages more 'user-friendly'. Their best approach, so far, has been to take all the old brochures, and stamp the words, 'user-friendly' on the cover.

Bill Gates, US computer engineer, entrepeneur (b. 1955)

I have a spelling checker
It came with my PC;
It plainly marks four my revue
Mistakes I cannot sea.
I've run this poem threw it,
I'm sure your pleased too no,
Its letter perfect in it's weigh,
My checker tolled me sew.

Janet Minor, US internet poet

A computer lets you make more mistakes faster than any invention in human history - with the possible exceptions of handguns and tequila.

Mitch Ratcliffe, US computer journalist

When all else fails, read the instructions.

Technological man can't believe in anything that can't be measured, taped, or put into a computer.

Claire Booth Luce, US author, polititian, diplomat (1903-1987)

CONTINUOUS IMPROVEMENT

He who stops being better stops being good.

Oliver Cromwell, English soldier, statesman (1599-1658)

There's only one corner of the universe you can be certain of improving, and that's your own self.

Aldous Huxley, British author (1894-1963)

It is necessary to try to surpass oneself always; this occupation ought to last as long as life.

Christina, Queen of Sweden (1632-1654)

The road to success is always under construction.

Jim Miller, US economist, politician (b. 1942)

We must not, in trying to think about how we can make a big difference, ignore the small daily differences we can make which, over time, add up to big differences that we often cannot foresee.

Marian Wright Edelman, US lawyer (b. 1939)

Great things are done by a series of small things brought together.

Vincent Van Gogh, Dutch painter (1853-1890)

There is no brilliant single stroke that is going to transform the water into wine or straw into gold.

Coleman Young, US senator (b. 1918)

You can't improve 100% in one thing. But you can improve 1% in 100 things.

J Willard Marriott, US executive, Marriott Hotels (b. 1932)

The rung of the ladder was never meant to rest upon, but only to hold a man's foot long enough to enable him to put the other somewhat higher.

T H Huxley, British biologist (1825-1895)

The productivity of people requires continuous learning, as the Japanese have taught us. It requires adoption in the West of the specific Japanese Zen concept where one learns to do better what one already does well.

Peter Drucker, US management author, consultant (b. 1909)

Improvement makes straight roads; but the crooked roads without improvement are roads of genius.

William Blake, British poet, painter, engraver (1757-1827)

Success is the sum of small efforts, repeated day in and day out.

Robert Collier, US advertising copywriter

Without continual growth and progress, such words as improvement, achievement, and success have no meaning.

Benjamin Franklin, US statesman, author, scientist (1706-1790)

Have no fear of perfection - you'll never reach it.

Salvador Dali, Spanish artist (1904-1989)

CONTRIBUTION

Life's most urgent question is: what are you doing for others?

Martin Luther King Jr, US civil rights leader (1929-1968)

If there be any truer measure of a man than by what he does, it must be by what he gives.

Robert South, English clergyman (1634-1716)

We are here on earth to do for others. What the others are here for, I don't know.

W H Auden, British poet (1907-1973)

From what we get, we can make a living; what we give, however, makes a life.

Arthur Ashe, US tennis player (1943-1993)

The simplest and shortest ethical precept is to be served as little as possible - and to serve others as much as possible.

Leo Tolstoy, Russian author (1828-1910)

It is one of the most beautiful compensations of this life that no man can sincerely try to help another without helping himself.

Ralph Waldo Emerson, American essayist, poet (1803-1882)

The miracle is this; the more we share, the more we have.

Leonard Nimoy, US actor (b. 1931)

No man, who continues to add something to the material, intellectual and moral well being of the place in which he lives, is left long without proper reward.

Booker T Washington, US reformer, teacher (1856-1915)

There was never a person who did anything worth doing that did not receive more than he gave.

Henry Ward Beecher, US preacher, author (1813-1887)

Beginning today, treat everyone you meet as if they were going to be dead by midnight. Extend to them all the care, kindness, and understanding you can muster, and do it with no thought of any reward. Your life will never be the same again.

Augustine (Og) Mandino, US insurance businessman, author (1923-1996)

For it is in giving that we receive.

Francis of Assisi, Italian friar (1182-1226)

CONTROL

You can't hold a man down without staying down with him.

Booker T Washington, US reformer, teacher (1856-1915)

You do not lead by hitting people over the head - that's assault, not leadership.

Dwight D Eisenhower, US President, general (1890-1969)

Those who can command themselves, command others.

William Hazlitt, British journalist, essayist (1778-1830)

People have changed. They know more, they want to know more, they expect more, they want to be more, they want to fill up their lives with work that has meaning. There's no time to worry about keeping everybody in line. Control is an illusion only achieved when people are controlling themselves.

David Firth, British management author (b. 1949)

COURAGE

Courage is one step ahead of fear.

Coleman Young, US senator (b. 1918)

Always do what you are afraid to do.

Ralph Waldo Emerson, American essayist, poet (1803-1882)

Far better to dare mighty things, to win glorious triumphs, even though checkered by failure, than to take rank with those poor spirits who neither enjoy much nor suffer much ... in the grey twilight that knows not victory nor defeat.

Theodore Roosevelt, US President (1858-1919)

You gain strength, courage and confidence by every experience in which you really stop to look fear in the face. You are able to say to yourself, 'I lived through this horror. I can take the next thing that comes along.' You must do the thing you think you cannot do.

Eleanor Roosevelt, US United Nations delegate (1884-1962)

The greater the difficulty the more glory in surmounting it. Skilful pilots gain their reputation from storms and tempests.

Epictetus, Greek philosopher (55-135 AD)

The bravest are surely those who have the clearest vision of what is before them, glory and danger alike, and yet notwithstanding, go out and meet it.

Pericles, Athenian statesman (495-429 BC)

A great deal of talent is lost to the world for want of a little courage.

Johann Wolfgang von Goethe, German poet, letter-writer (1749-1832)

Sometimes you just have to take the leap, and build your wings on the way down.

Kobi Yamada

Security is mostly superstition. It does not exist in nature, nor do the children of men as a whole experience it. Avoidance of danger is not safer in the long run than outright exposure. Life is either a daring adventure, or nothing.

Helen Keller, US writer, lecturer (1880-1968)

It is better to err on the side of daring than the side of caution.

Alvin Toffler, US management author, editor (b. 1928)

Whenever you see a successful business, someone once made a courageous decision.

Peter Drucker, US management author, consultant (b. 1909)

Success is not final, failure is not fatal: it is the courage to continue that counts.

Winston Churchill, British Prime Minister (1874-1965)

Efforts and courage are not enough without purpose and direction.

John F Kennedy, US President (1917-1963)

Courage is the main quality of leadership, in my opinion: courage to initiate something and keep it going - pioneering an adventurous spirit to blaze new ways.

Walt Disney, US artist, film producer (1901-1966)

Let me win, but if I cannot win, let me be brave in the attempt.

Special Olympics Motto

CREATIVITY

A hunch is creativity trying to tell you something.

Frank Capra, Italian/US film director (1897-1991)

Confusion is the welcome mat at the door of creativity.

Michael J Gelb, US author, educator (b. 1952)

Creativity is a type of learning process where the teacher and pupil are located in the same individual.

Arthur Koestler, British author (1905-1983)

Why do we only ever play these games - games that are designed to stimulate us, to solve differences and to make us think creatively - in the training room?

David Firth, British management author (b. 1949)

Think before you speak is criticism's motto: speak before you think, creation's.

E M Forster, British author (1879-1970)

Creativity is the ability to see relationships where none exist.

Thomas Disch, US author (b. 1940)

Storm and Silence - the two modes of group creativity. Together they unlock a world of rich inspiration.

David Williams, British management author, presenter (b. 1950)

CRITICISM

To knock a thing down, especially if it is cocked at an arrogant angle, is a deep delight of the blood.

George Santayana, US philosopher, poet (1863-1952)

Honest criticism is hard to take, particularly from a relative, a friend an acquaintance, or a stranger.

Franklin P Jones

I can take any amount of criticism, so long as it is unqualified praise.

Noel Coward, British actor, playwright, composer (1899-1973)

We swallow greedily any lie that flatters us, but we sip only little by little at a truth we find bitter.

Denis Diderot, French philosopher (1713-1784)

Great spirits have always encountered violent opposition from mediocre minds.

Albert Einstein, German physicist (1879-1955)

Too many of us take pleasure in discouraging people by pointing out their mistakes and getting excited about their failures rather than focusing on their strengths and getting excited about their possibilities.

John C Maxwell, US clergyman, author

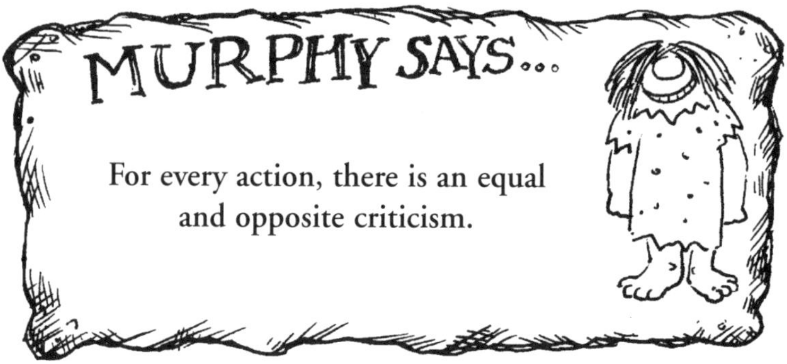

People spend too much time finding other people to blame, too much energy finding excuses for not being what they are capable of being, and not enough energy putting themselves on the line, growing out of the past, and getting on with their lives.

J Michael Straczynski, US science fiction writer, producer

Evaluation of performance, merit rating, or annual review nourishes short-term performance, annihilates long term planning, builds fear, demolishes teamwork, nourishes rivalry and politics. It leaves people bitter, crushed, bruised, battered, desolate, despondent, dejected, feeling inferior, some even depressed, unfit for work for weeks after receipt of rating, unable to comprehend why they are inferior.

W Edwards Deming, US statistician, author (1900-1993)

Don't find fault, find a remedy.

Henry Ford, US automobile manufacturer, engineer (1863-1947)

CURIOSITY

When a finger points to the moon the imbecile looks at the finger.

Zen koan

Curiosity is one of the most permanent and certain characteristics of a vigorous mind.

Samuel Johnson, British poet, critic, lexicographer (1709-1784)

The important thing is not to stop questioning. Curiosity has its own reason for existing. One cannot help but be in awe when he contemplates the mysteries of eternity, of life, of the marvellous structure of reality. It is enough if one tries merely to comprehend a little of this mystery every day. Never lose a holy curiosity.

Albert Einstein, German physicist (1879-1955)

I roamed the countryside searching for the answers to things I did not understand. Why shells existed on the tops of mountains along with the imprints of coral and plant and seaweed usually found in the sea. Why the thunder lasts a longer time that that which causes it and why immediately on its creation the lightning becomes visible to the eye while thunder requires time to travel. How the various circles of water form around the spot which has been struck by a stone and why a bird sustains itself in the air. These questions and other strange phenomena engaged my thought throughout my life.

Leonarda da Vinci, Italian painter, sculptor, architect, engineer (1452-1519)

Men go abroad to wonder at the height of mountains, at the huge waves of the sea, at the long courses of the rivers, at the vast compass of the ocean, at the circular motions of the stars; and they pass by themselves without wondering.

St Augustine, Latin scholar, high priest (354-430 AD)

We keep moving forward, opening up new doors, and doing new things, because we're curious - and curiosity keeps leading us down new paths.

Walt Disney, US artist, film producer (1901-1966)

Change pace. Go to work next Thursday and declare it miniature golf-day. Showing a training film this afternoon? Order popcorn for every participant. Curiosity has a lot to do with looking at the world through slightly cockeyed glasses.

Tom Peters, US management author, presenter (b. 1942)

I like to think that I walk through life with my eyebrows continually raised.

Warren Bennis, US academic, management author (b. 1925)

Curiosity is the wick in the candle of learning.

William Ward, British author, theologian (1812-1882)

Complacency is the enemy of curiosity.

Charles Handy, British management consultant, author (b. 1924)

CUSTOMERS

It is not the employer who pays the wages. Employers only handle money. It is the customer who pays the wages.

Henry Ford, US automobile manufacturer, engineer (1863-1947)

Companies can't give job security, only customers can.

Jack Welch, US executive, utility chief (b. 1935)

Consumers are statistics. Customers are people.

Stanley Marcus, retail executive (b. 1905)

To please people is a great step towards persuading them.

Philip Dormer Stanhope, British statesman (1694-1774)

In the age of e-mail, supercomputer power on the desktop, the Internet, and the raucous global village, *attentiveness* - a token of human kindness - is the greatest gift we can give someone.

Tom Peters, US management author, presenter (b. 1942)

It is not your client's or prospect's job to remember you. It is your responsibility to make sure they do not have the chance to forget you.

Patricia Fripp, US management consultant

No matter what strategy leaders inside the organisation devise, what customers see is at the front line.

Rosabeth Moss Kanter, US academic, management author (b. 1943)

The customer is a rear-view mirror, not a guide to the future.

George Colony, US research head

Don't just ask what your customers want. Think ahead of them and create what they didn't know they wanted.

David Williams, British management author, presenter (b. 1950)

Good will, like a good name, is got by many actions and lost by one.

Lord Jeffrey, British literary critic, judge (1773-1850)

An untreated complaint is like an untreated wound; it festers and gets worse.

Geoff Burch, British management author, presenter (b. 1951)

The next time you face a customer who has every right to be upset, say something like this: 'I don't blame you for feeling as you do. If I were you, I'd feel exactly the same way. What would you like for me to do?' These are magical, healing words, and you'll be surprised at how reasonable people become when they believe you are on their side.

H Jackson Brown Jr, US author, moralist

Your customer has one fundamental reason for doing business with you; so that he himself can do more business.

David Bland

DISCOVERY

The only real voyage of discovery consists not in seeking new landscapes but in having new eyes.

Marcel Proust, French author (1871-1922)

It is by logic that we prove, but by intuition that we discover.

Henri Poincare, French mathematician (1854-1912)

No great discovery was ever made without a bold guess.

Sir Isaac Newton, English physicist, mathematician (1642-1727)

Discovery consists of seeing what everybody has seen and thinking what nobody has thought.

Albert von Szent-Gyorgyi, US biochemist (1893-1986)

One of the advantages of being disorderly is that one is constantly making exciting discoveries.

A A Milne, British author (1882-1956)

The more original a discovery, the more obvious it seems afterwards.

Arthur Koestler, British author (1905-1983)

It will come unexpectedly from the depths of tortured silence in a shot of sudden exhilaration - that Eureka moment.

David Williams, British management author, presenter (b. 1950)

The only way round is through.

Robert Frost, US poet (1874-1963)

The greatest obstacle to discovery is not ignorance - it is the illusion of knowledge.

Daniel J Boorstin, US media author, historian (b. 1914)

DOUBT

The only limit to our realisation of tomorrow will be our doubts of today.

Franklin D Roosevelt, US President (1882-1945)

Doubt is not a pleasant condition, but certainty is absurd.

Voltaire, French philosopher (1694-1778)

I love to doubt as well as know.

Dante, Italian poet (1265-1321)

Tell people there are more than 300,000 billion stars in the universe and they will believe you without question. Tell them a porch railing has wet paint on it and they have to touch it to make sure.

Jaeger

If you would be a real seeker after truth, it is necessary that at least once in your life you doubt, as far as possible, all things.

René Descartes, French philosopher (1596-1650)

Our doubts are traitors and make us lose the good we oft might win, by fearing to attempt.

William Shakespeare, English playwright, poet (1564-1616)

DREAMS

Everything starts as somebody's daydream.

Larry Niven, US science fiction author (b. 1938)

You see things and you say 'Why?' But I dream things that never were and say 'Why not?'

George Bernard Shaw, Irish playwright, essayist (1856-1950)

I used to think as I looked out on the Hollywood night, 'There must be thousands of girls sitting alone like me, dreaming of becoming a movie star.' But I'm not going to worry about them. I'm dreaming the hardest.

Marilyn Monroe, US actress (1926-1962)

I like the dreams of the future better than the history of the past.

Thomas Jefferson, US President (1741-1826)

The future belongs to those who believe in the beauty of their dreams.

Eleanor Roosevelt, US United Nations delegate (1884-1962)

If you can dream it, you can do it.

Walt Disney, US artist, film producer (1901-1966)

It may be those who dream most do most.

Stephen Leacock, British-born Canadian humorist (1869-1944)

Our life is composed greatly from dreams, from the unconscious, and they must be brought into connection with action. They must be woven together.

Anais Nin, US author (1903-1977)

Dreams come true; without that possibility, nature would not incite us to have them.

John Updike, US author (b. 1932)

We grow great by dreams. All big men are dreamers. They see things in the soft haze of a spring day or in the red fire of a long winter's evening. Some of us let these great dreams die, but others nourish and protect them, nurse them through bad days till they bring them to the sunshine and light which comes always to those who sincerely hope that their dreams will come true.

Woodrow Wilson, US President (1856-1924)

Rose-coloured glasses are never made in bifocals. Nobody wants to read the small print in dreams.

Ann Landers, US advice columnist (b. 1918)

Dare to be wrong and to dream.

Friedrich von Schiller, German dramatist, poet (1759-1805)

Those who dream by day are cognisant of many things which escape those who dream only by night.

Edgar Allan Poe, US poet, novelist (1809-1849)

Dreamers exist to keep the dreams alive until the non-dreamers are ready to dream.

Pierre LeClerc, French management consultant

If you have built castles in the air, your work need not be lost; that is where they should be. Now put the foundations under them.

Henry David Thoreau, US essayist, poet (1817-1862)

The things that haven't been done before,
Those are the things to try;
Columbus dreamed of an unknown shore
At the rim of the far-flung sky.

Edgar Albert Guest, US poet (1881-1959)

It isn't a calamity to die with dreams unfulfilled, but it is a calamity not to dream.

Benjamin Elijah Mays, US clergyman, author (1895-1984)

I prefer to be a dreamer among the humblest, with visions to be realised, than lord among those without dreams and desires.

Kahlil Gibran, Lebanese philosopher, author, poet (1883-1931)

EDUCATION

If you give a man a fish, he will have a single meal. If you teach him how to fish, he will eat all his life.

Kwan-Tzu

If you are planning for a year, sow rice; if you are planning for a decade, plant trees; if you are planning for a lifetime, educate people.

Chinese proverb

Education is our passport to the future, for tomorrow belongs to the people who prepare for it today.

Malcolm X, American civil rights activist (1926-1965)

Education is the most powerful weapon which you can use to change the world.

Nelson Mandela, South African statesman (b. 1918)

Education's purpose is to replace an empty mind with an open one.

Malcolm S Forbes, US publisher, media magnate

Everybody is ignorant, only on different subjects.

Will Rogers, US actor, humorist (1879-1935)

If you think education is expensive - try ignorance.

Derek Bok, US protector of law (b. 1930)

Education makes people easy to lead, but difficult to drive; easy to govern, but impossible to enslave.

Henry Peter Brougham, Scottish jurist, politician (1778-1868)

It is the mark of an educated mind to be able to entertain a thought without accepting it.

Aristotle, Greek philosopher, scientist, physician (384-322 BC)

The only thing that interferes with my learning is my education.

Albert Einstein, German physicist (1879-1955)

It is, in fact, nothing short of a miracle that the modern methods of instruction have not yet entirely strangled the holy curiosity of inquiry.

Albert Einstein, German physicist (1879-1955)

What we want is to see the child in pursuit of knowledge, and not knowledge in pursuit of the child.

George Bernard Shaw, Irish playwright, essayist (1856-1950)

When a subject becomes totally obsolete we make it a required course.

Peter Drucker, US management author, consultant (b. 1909)

Formal education will make you a living; self-education will make you a fortune.

Jim Rohn, US motivational speaker, author

Learning you get from school. Education you get from life.

Mark Twain, US author (1835-1910)

Every man who rises above the common level has received two educations: the first from his teachers; the second, more personal and important, from himself.

Edward Gibbon, British historian (1737-1794)

He that is taught only by himself has a fool for a master.

Ben Jonson, English dramatist, poet (1572-1637)

One looks back with appreciation to the brilliant teachers, but with gratitude to those who touched our human feeling.

Carl Gustav Jung, Swiss psychiatrist, analytical psychologist (1876-1961)

A teacher affects eternity. He can never tell where his influence stops.

Henry Adams, US historian (1838-1918)

The mediocre teacher tells. The good teacher explains. The superior teacher demonstrates. The great teacher inspires.

William Ward, British author, theologian (1812-1882)

Education would be so much more effective if its purpose were to ensure that by the time they leave school every boy and girl should know how much they don't know, and be imbued with a lifetime desire to know it.

Sir William Haley, British editor, Director General of the BBC (1901-1987)

Teachers open the door, but you must enter by yourself.

Chinese proverb

Everybody should have an equal chance - but all should have a flying start.

Harold Wilson, British Prime Minister (1916-1995)

Human history becomes more and more a race between education and catastrophe.

H G Wells, British author, journalist (1866-1946)

We have to abandon the idea that schooling is something restricted to youth. How can it be, in a world where half the things a man knows at 20 are no longer true at 40 - and half the things he knows at 40 hadn't been discovered when he was 20?

Arthur C Clarke, British author (b. 1917)

Education can no longer be confined to the schools. Every employing institution has to become a teacher.

Peter Drucker, US management author, consultant (b. 1909)

The entire object of true education is to make people not merely do the right thing, but to enjoy right things; not merely industrious, but to love industry; not merely learned, but to love knowledge.

John Ruskin, British writer, art critic (1819-1900)

A lot of fellows nowadays have a B.A., M.D., or Ph.D. Unfortunately, they don't have a J.O.B.

'Fats' Domino, US singer, pianist, composer (b. 1928)

EMPOWERMENT

Almost every organisation I have ever worked with claims to place a high value on empowerment. Almost none really means it.

Will Schutz, US author (b. 1925)

A leader must not only be willing to give opportunity to others, but must be in the business of creating opportunity for others.

William Hodges, US federal judge (b. 1934)

Don't tell people how to do things. Tell them what to do and let them surprise you with their results.

George S Patton, US general (1885-1945)

Surround yourself with the best people you can find, delegate authority, and don't interfere.

Ronald Reagan, US President, actor (b. 1911)

You cannot mandate productivity, you must provide the tools to let people become their best.

Steve Jobs, US executive, co-founder of Apple Computer Inc (b. 1955)

The best executive is one who has sense enough to pick good people to do what he wants them to do, and self-restraint enough to keep from meddling with them while they do it.

Theodore Roosevelt, US President (1858-1919)

Here lies a man who knew how to enlist the service of better men than himself.

Tombstone of Andrew Carnegie, Scottish industrialist, philanthropist (1835-1919)

The ultimate leader is one who is willing to develop people to the point that they surpass him or her in knowledge and ability.

Fred A Manske Jr

The ultimate motivational empowerment question:
Could you show me how to do that?

David Firth, British management author (b. 1949)

Proper leadership empowers the workforce. An empowered workforce means one that's committed, that feels that they're learning, that they're competent. They have a sense of human bond, a sense of community, a sense of meaning in their work.

Warren Bennis, US academic, management author (b. 1925)

As the walls come down, we can master change by sharing a common set of goals and purposes, by giving people the data they need so they can guide and direct their own actions.

Rosabeth Moss Kanter, US academic, management author (b. 1943)

Participation is not empowerment.

Daniel Quinn Mills, US academic, management author (b. 1941)

ENCOURAGEMENT

If you would lift me you must be on higher ground.

Ralph Waldo Emerson, American essayist, poet (1803-1882)

Those who are lifting the world upward and onward are those who encourage more than criticise.

Elizabeth Harrison, US educator (1849-1927)

Material things aside, we need no advice but approval.

Coco Chanel, French fashion designer (1883-1971)

Correction does much, but encouragement does more. Encouragement after censure is as the sun after a shower.

Johann Wolfgang von Goethe, German poet, letter-writer (1749-1832)

There is no such thing as a 'self-made' man. We are made up of thousands of others. Everyone who has ever done a kind deed for us, or spoken one word of encouragement to us, has entered into the make-up of our character and of our thoughts, as well as our success.

George Matthew Adams, US newspaper magnate

Flatter me, and I may not believe you. Criticise me and I may not like you. Ignore me, and I may not forgive you. Encourage me, and I will not forget you.

William Ward, British author, theologian (1812-1882)

Keep away from people who try to belittle your ambitions. Small people always do that, but the really great make you feel that you, too, can become great.

Mark Twain, US author (1835-1910)

ENTHUSIASM

The real secret of success is enthusiasm.

Walter Chrysler, US businessman, founder of Chrysler Corporation (1875-1940)

If you can give your son or daughter only one gift, let it be enthusiasm.

Bruce Barton, US author, advertising executive (1886-1967)

Enthusiasm is the electricity of life. How do you get it? You act enthusiastic until you make it a habit.

Gordon Parks, US film director, photographer, author (b. 1912)

You can do anything if you have enthusiasm. Enthusiasm is the yeast that makes your hopes rise to the stars. With it, there is accomplishment. Without it there are only alibis.

Henry Ford, US automobile manufacturer, engineer (1863-1947)

A man can succeed at almost everything for which he has unlimited enthusiasm.

Charles Schwab, US industrialist (1862-1939)

Flaming enthusiasm, backed by horse sense and persistence, is the quality that most frequently makes for success.

Dale Carnegie, US lecturer, author (1888-1955)

You can't sweep people off their feet if you can't be swept off your own.

Clarence Day, US author (1874-1935)

Leadership is leaving zest in your wake.

Tom Peters, US management author, presenter (b. 1942)

Every production of genius must be the production of enthusiasm.

Benjamin Disraeli, British Prime Minister (1804-1881)

The man who feels no enthusiasm for his work will never accomplish anything worthwhile.

Sir William C Van Horne, Canadian railway magnate

No person who is enthusiastic about his work has anything to fear from life.

Samuel Goldwyn, Polish-born US film producer (1882-1974)

Every great and commanding moment in the annals of the world is the triumph of somebody's enthusiasm.

Ralph Waldo Emerson, American essayist, poet (1803-1882)

There is a real magic in enthusiasm. It spells the difference between mediocrity and accomplishment.

Norman Vincent Peale, US author, clergyman (1898-1993)

One man has enthusiasm for 30 minutes, another for 30 days, but it is the man who has it for 30 years who makes a success of life.

Edward B Butler, US scientist

Keep your face to the sunshine and you cannot see the shadow.

Helen Keller, US writer, lecturer (1880-1968)

The world is full of willing people, some willing to work, the rest willing to let them.

Robert Frost, US poet (1874-1963)

If you aren't fired with enthusiasm, you will be fired with enthusiasm.

Vince Lombardi, US football coach (1913-1970)

What America needs is more young people who will carry to their jobs the same enthusiasm for getting ahead that they display in traffic.

M A Kelly

We act as though comfort and luxury were the chief requirements of life, when all that we need to make us happy is something to be enthusiastic about.

Charles Kingsley, British clergyman, author (1819-1879)

ENVIRONMENT

It isn't pollution that's harming the environment. It's the impurities in our air and water that are doing it.

Dan Quayle, US Vice President (b. 1947)

Any fine morning a power saw can fell a tree that took a thousand years to grow.

Edwin Way Teale, US naturalist, photographer (1899-1980)

We do not inherit this land from our ancestors; we borrow it from our children.

Haida Indian saying

A society grows great when old men plant trees whose shade they know they shall never sit in.

Greek proverb

The best use of life is to spend it for something that outlasts life.

William James, US philosopher, psychologist (1842-1910)

EXCELLENCE

Be the best. If others don't see it, who cares?

Oprah Winfrey, US talk show host, actress (b. 1954)

You do not merely want to be considered just the best of the best. You want to be considered the only ones who do what you do.

Jerry Garcia, US rock musician (1942-1995)

It takes a long time to bring excellence to maturity.

Titus Livy, Roman historian (59 BC-17 AD)

Infinite striving to be the best is man's duty, it is its own reward. Everything else is in God's hands.

Mahatma Gandhi, Indian nationalist leader (1869-1948)

Learn to say 'no' to the good so you can say 'yes' to the best.

John C Maxwell, US clergyman, author

The quality of a person's life is in direct proportion to their commitment to excellence, regardless of their chosen field of endeavour.

Vince Lombardi, US football coach (1913-1970)

The society that scorns excellence in plumbing because plumbing is a humble activity, and tolerates shoddiness in philosophy because philosophy is an exalted activity, will have neither good plumbing nor good philosophy. Neither its pipes nor its theories will hold water.

John Gardner, US writer, educator (b. 1912)

Striving for excellence motivates you; striving for perfection is demoralising.

Harriet Braiker, US psychologist, management consultant (b. 1948)

Demand perfection of yourself and you'll seldom attain it. Fear of making a mistake is the biggest single cause of making one. Relax - pursue excellence, not perfection.

Bud Winter, US sprint coach (1909-1985)

If you don't do it excellently, don't do it at all. Because if it's not excellent, it won't be profitable or fun, and if you're not in business for fun or profit, what the hell are you doing there?

Robert Townsend, US author, businessman (1920-1998)

FACILITATION

A Zen master once asked an audience of Westerners what they thought was the most important word in the English language. After giving his listeners the chance to think about such favourite words as love, truth, failure and so on, he said, 'No, it's a three letter word: it's the word *let*. Let it be. Let it happen.'

W Timothy Gallwey, US author

There are two ways of being creative. One can sing and dance. Or one can create an environment in which singers and dancers flourish.

Warren Bennis, US academic, management author (b. 1925)

What we call leadership consists mainly of knowing how to follow. The wise leader stays in the background and facilitates other people's processes.

John Heider, US management author

There are no problem people, only problem facilitators, who can't cope with energy and creativity.

Trevor Bentley, US facilitator, author

FACTS

Get the facts, or the facts will get you. And when you get 'em, get 'em right, or they will get you wrong.

Thomas Fuller, English preacher, scholar, author (1608-1661)

Get your facts first, then you can distort them as you please.

Mark Twain, US author (1835-1910)

Facts are stubborn things; and whatever may be our wishes, our inclinations, or the dictates of our passions, they cannot alter the state of facts and evidence.

John Quincy Adams, US President (1767-1848)

Facts do not cease to exist because they are ignored.

Aldous Huxley, British author (1894-1963)

He uses statistics as a drunken man uses lamp-posts - for support rather than illumination.

Andrew Lang, Scottish author (1844-1912)

We want the facts to fit the preconceptions. When they don't, it is easier to ignore the facts than to change the preconceptions.

Jessamyn West, US novelist (1903-1984)

People don't ask for facts in making up their minds. They would rather have one good, soul-satisfying emotion than a dozen facts.

Robert Keith Leavitt

No great marketing decisions have ever been made on quantitative data.

John Sculley, US businessman, computers & drinks (b. 1939)

Information is pretty thin stuff unless mixed with experience.

Clarence Day, US author (1874-1935)

It is the spirit of the age to believe that any fact, however suspect, is superior to any imaginative exercise, no matter how true.

Gore Vidal, US author, essayist (b. 1925)

FAILURE

If you're not failing every now and again, it's a sign you're not doing anything very innovative.

Woody Allen, US film actor, director (b. 1935)

The most important of my discoveries have been suggested to me by my failures.

Humphrey Davy, British chemist (1778-1829)

Failure is, in a sense, the highway to success.

John Keats, British poet (1795-1821)

All of us failed to match our dreams of perfection. So I rate us on the basis of our splendid failure to do the impossible.

William Faulkner, US author (1897-1962)

There could be no honour in a sure success, but much might be wrested from a sure defeat.

T E Lawrence, British soldier, author, aka *Lawrence of Arabia (1888-1935)*

Our greatest glory is not in never failing, but in rising every time we fail.

Confucius, Chinese philosopher, teacher (551-479 BC)

Failures are like skinned knees - painful, but superficial.

H Ross Perot, US executive, Presidential candidate (b. 1930)

If you have made mistakes, there is always another chance for you. You may have a fresh start any moment you choose, for this thing we call 'failure' is not the falling down, but the staying down.

Mary Pickford, US actress (1893-1979)

There's only one way you can fail, and that's to quit.

B C Forbes, Scottish journalist (1880-1954)

If you want to succeed, double your failure rate.

Thomas J Watson, US businessman, founder of IBM (1874-1956)

I have always believed, and I still believe, that whatever good or bad fortune may come our way we can always give it meaning and transform it into something of value.

Hermann Hesse, German author, poet (1877-1962)

Failing is good, as long as it doesn't become a habit.

Michael Eisner, US executive, Walt Disney Corporation (b. 1942)

Failure is the opportunity to begin again more intelligently.

Henry Ford, US automobile manufacturer, engineer (1863-1947)

Do not be too timid and squeamish about your actions. All life is an experiment. The more experiments you make the better. What if they are a little coarse, and you may get your coat soiled or torn? What if you do fail, and get fairly rolled in the dirt once or twice. Up again, you shall never be so afraid of a tumble.

Ralph Waldo Emerson, American essayist, poet (1803-1882)

A man fails many times but he isn't a failure until he begins to blame somebody else.

J Paul Getty, US businessman (1892-1976)

An inventor fails 999 times, and if he succeeds once, he's in. He treats his failures simply as practice shots.

Charles Kettering, US engineer, inventor (1876-1958)

The way I see it, if you want the rainbow, you gotta put up with some rain.

Dolly Parton, US singer, actress (b. 1946)

To err is human; to blame it on the other guy is even more human.

Bob Goddard, US physicist, rocketry pioneer (1882-1945)

A man who smiles when things go wrong has thought of someone he can blame it on.

Notice the difference between what happens when a man says to himself, 'I have failed three times,' and what happens when he says, 'I am a failure.'

S I Hayakawa, Canadian scholar, senator (1906-1992)

If at first you don't succeed, failure may be your style.

Quentin Crisp, British author (b. 1908)

Half the failures in life arise from pulling in one's horse as it is leaping.

Julius Hare, British author (1795-1855)

I don't measure a man's success by how high he climbs but how high he bounces when he hits bottom.

George S Patton, US general (1885-1945)

FOCUS

If you have 25 priorities, you have none. And if you don't know it, your customers do.

Jan Carlson, Scandinavian airlines executive

There is nothing so useless as doing efficiently that which should not be done at all.

Peter Drucker, US management author, consultant (b. 1909)

Suppose you were taking a course in parachuting and there were 100 things to learn to do successfully. You correctly identified 99 of these 100 items on the written test. But on your first jump, you couldn't remember how to pull the rip cord, which was the item you missed. You'd probably earn a posthumous A for the course from most teachers, but it wouldn't bring you back from the dead. If you want to jump safely, worry less about your test score and worry about what's important and what's not. Then learn and do the important things.

Wess Roberts, US author (b. 1946)

Those who cannot tell what they desire or expect, still sigh and struggle with indefinite thoughts and vast wishes.

Ralph Waldo Emerson, American essayist, poet (1803-1882)

Anyone can do any amount of work provided it isn't the work he is supposed to be doing at that moment.

Robert Benchley, US humourist (1889-1945)

FUN

Work should be more fun than fun.

Noel Coward, British actor, playwright, composer (1899-1973)

The man who does not work for the love of work but only for money is not likely to make money nor find much fun in life.

Charles Schwab, US industrialist (1862-1939)

Serious-minded people have few ideas. People with ideas are never serious.

Paul Valery, French poet, critic (1871-1945)

Make a resolution not to become suspicious when you hear people laughing.

David Firth, British management author (b. 1949)

Laughter is the shortest distance between two people.

Victor Borge, Danish entertainer, pianist (b. 1909)

First you have to have fun. Second, you have to put love where your labour is. Third, you have to go in the opposite direction to everyone else.

Anita Roddick, British executive, founder of The Body Shop (b. 1943)

If people never did silly things nothing intelligent would ever get done.

Ludwig Wittgenstein, Austrian philosopher (1889-1951)

A little nonsense now and then, is cherished by the wisest men.

Willy Wonka, character in 'Charlie and the Chocolate Factory' by Roald Dahl (1916-1990)

We're all working harder and faster. But unless we're also having fun the transformation doesn't work.

Jack Welch, US executive, utility chief (b. 1935)

I like nonsense, it wakes up the brain cells. Fantasy is a necessary ingredient in living, it's a way of looking at life through the wrong end of a telescope and that enables you to laugh at life's realities.

Geisel Theodor Seuss aka *Dr Seuss, US author (1904-1991)*

The one serious conviction that a man should have is that nothing is to be taken too seriously.

Nicholas Butler, US educator, Nobel Peace Prize winner (1862-1947)

Seriousness is the only refuge of the shallow.

Oscar Wilde, Irish dramatist, poet (1854-1900)

FUTURE

Remember, today is the tomorrow you worried about yesterday.

Dale Carnegie, US lecturer, author (1888-1955)

My interest is in the future because I'm going to spend the rest of my life there.

Charles F Kettering, US engineer (1876-1958)

The best way to be ready for the future is to invent it.

John Sculley, US businessman, computers & drinks (b. 1939)

Your successful past will block your visions of the future.

Joel Barker, US management author, presenter

The future belongs to those who believe in the beauty of their dreams.

Eleanor Roosevelt, US United Nations delegate (1884-1962)

The future is like heaven - everyone exalts it but no one wants to go there now.

James Baldwin, US author (1924-1987)

The future has a habit of suddenly and dramatically becoming the present.

Roger W Babson, US statistician, columnist (1875-1967)

The past cannot be changed, the future is still in your power.

Hugh White, US politician (1773-1840)

No sensible decision can be made any longer without taking into account not only the world as it is, but the world as it will be.

Isaac Asimov, Russian biochemist, author (1920-1992)

Tomorrow is often the busiest time of the year.

Business, more than any other occupation, is a continual dealing with the future; it is a continual calculation, an instinctive exercise in foresight.

Henry R Luce, US publisher (1898-1967)

The ability to plan for what has not yet happened, for a future that has only been imagined, is one of the hallmarks of leadership.

Warren Bennis, US academic, management author (b. 1925)

Those who talk about the future are scoundrels. It is the present that matters.

Louis Ferdinand Céline, French novelist (1894-1961)

As for the future, your task is not to foresee but to enable it.

Antoine De Saint-Éxupéry, French author (1900-1944)

GENIUS

One machine can do the work of fifty ordinary men. No machine can do the work of one extraordinary man.

Elbert Hubbard, US publisher, editor (1856-1915)

Genius is that energy which collects, combines, amplifies and animates.

Samuel Johnson, British poet, critic, lexicographer (1709-1784)

It takes a lot of time to be a genius; you have to sit around so much doing nothing, really doing nothing.

Gertrude Stein, US author (1874-1946)

When a true genius appears in the world, you may know him by this sign, that the dunces are all in confederacy against him.

Jonathan Swift, Irish clergyman, poet, satirist (1667-1745)

In the republic of mediocrity, genius is dangerous.

Robert G Ingersoll, US politician, orator (1833-1899)

Jealousy is the tribute mediocrity pays to genius.

Fulton John Sheen, US catholic clergyman, evangelist (1895-1979)

Genius begins great works; labour alone finishes them.

Joseph Joubert, French essayist, moralist (1754-1824)

Genius, in truth, means little more than the faculty of perceiving in an unhabitual way.

William James, US philosopher, psychologist (1842-1910)

Talent is that which is in a man's power; genius is that in whose power a man is.

James Russell Lowell, US poet, critic, statesman (1819-1891)

Towering genius disdains a beaten path. It seeks regions hitherto unexplored.

Abraham Lincoln, US President (1809-1865)

Adversity reveals genius, prosperity conceals it.

Horace, Roman poet, satirist (65 BC-8 BC)

Innovators and men of genius have almost always been regarded as fools at the beginning (and very often at the end) of their careers.

Fedor Dostoevsky, Russian author (1821-1881)

HABIT

Forgive him, for he believes that the customs of his tribe are the laws of nature.

George Bernard Shaw, Irish playwright, essayist (1856-1950)

If you have always done it that way, it's probably wrong.

Charles Kettering, US engineer, inventor (1876-1958)

If you always do what you've always done, you'll always get what you've always got.

Ed Foreman, US politician, entrepreneur (b. 1933)

New opinions are always suspected and usually opposed, without any other reason but because they are not already common.

John Locke, English philosopher (1632-1704)

It is hard to let old beliefs go. They are familiar. We are comfortable with them and have spent years building systems and developing habits that depend on them. Like a man who has worn eyeglasses so long that he forgets he has them on, we forget that the world looks to us the way it does because we have become used to seeing it that way through a particular set of lenses. Today, however, we need new lenses. And we need to throw the old ones away.

Kenich Ohmae, Japanese management consultant

It seems, in fact, as though the second half of a man's life is made up of nothing but the habits he has accumulated during the first half.

Fedor Dostoevsky, Russian author (1821-1881)

Conventional people are roused to fury by departure from convention, largely because they regard such departure as criticism of themselves.

Bertrand Russell, British philosopher, mathematician (1872-1970)

We are what we repeatedly do. Excellence then, is not an act, but a habit.

Aristotle, Greek philosopher, scientist, physician (384-322 BC)

It is never too late to give up your prejudices.

Henry David Thoreau, US essayist, poet (1817-1862)

IDEAS

If you want to have a great idea, have lots of ideas.

Linus Pauling, US chemist (1901-1994)

If I have a thousand ideas and only one turns out to be good, I am satisfied.

Alfred Nobel, Swedish chemist, businessman (1833-1896)

If at first the idea is not absurd, then there is no hope for it.

Albert Einstein, German physicist (1879-1955)

The need to be right all the time is the biggest bar to new ideas. It is better to have enough ideas for some of them to be wrong than to be always right by having no ideas at all.

Edward de Bono, Maltese psychologist, writer (b. 1933)

The idea that is not dangerous is not worthy of being called an idea at all.

Elbert Hubbard, US publisher, editor (1856-1915)

Daring ideas are like chessmen moved forward; they may be beaten, but they may start a winning game.

Johann Wolfgang von Goethe, German poet, letter-writer (1749-1832)

You can't crush ideas by suppressing them. You can only crush them by ignoring them.

Ursula K Le Guin, US author (b. 1929)

You cannot put a rope around the neck of an idea; you cannot put an idea up against the barrack-square wall and riddle it with bullets; you cannot confine it in the strongest prison cell your slaves could ever build.

Sean O'Casey, Irish dramatist, nationalist (1880-1964)

A new idea is delicate. It can be killed by a sneer or a yawn; it can be stabbed to death by a joke or worried to death by a frown on the right person's brow.

Charles Brower, US explorer, adventurer (1863-1945)

Lack of money is no obstacle. Lack of an idea is an obstacle.

Ken Hakuta

An idea, to be suggestive, must come to the individual with the force of revelation.

William James, US philosopher, psychologist (1842-1910)

New ideas can be good and bad, just the same as old ones.

Franklin D Roosevelt, US President (1882-1945)

Ideas are the raw material of progress. Everything first takes shape in the form of an idea. But an idea by itself is worth nothing. An idea, like a machine, must have power applied to it before it can accomplish anything.

B C Forbes, Scottish journalist (1880-1954)

The barriers to innovation in many companies are social as much as they are organisational; whole categories of people are ignored as sources of ideas.

Rosabeth Moss Kanter, US academic, management author (b. 1943)

If you want to get an idea across, wrap it up in a person.

Ralph Bunche, US diplomat (1904-1971)

A man may die, nations may rise and fall, but an idea lives on. Ideas have endurance without death.

John F Kennedy, US President (1917-1963)

Between the idea
and the reality
falls the shadow.

T S Eliot, US/British author, critic, dramatist (1888-1965)

IMAGES

What concerns me is not the way things are, but rather the way people think things are.

Epictetus, Greek philosopher (55-135 AD)

Things do not pass for what they are, but for what they seem. Most things are judged by their jackets.

Baltasar, Spanish philosopher, author (1601-1658)

We don't see things as they are, we see things as we are.

Anais Nin, US author (1903-1977)

An image is not simply a trademark, a design, a slogan or an easily remembered picture. It is a studiously crafted personality profile of an individual, institution, corporation, product or service.

Daniel J Boorstin, US media author, historian (b. 1914)

The right name is an advertisement in itself.

Claude C Hopkins, US advertising guru

Tell them it's Old Crow. Then give them another taste of Old Crow, but tell them it's Jack Daniels. Ask them which they prefer. They'll think the two drinks are quite different. They are tasting images.

David Ogilvy, US advertising executive, author (b. 1911)

There are always two people in every picture: the photographer and the viewer.

Ansel Adams, US photographer (1902-1984)

IMAGINATION

Imagination rules the world.

Napoleon Bonaparte, French soldier, statesman, revolutionary (1769-1821)

Imagination is more important than knowledge.

Albert Einstein, German physicist (1879-1955)

Everything you can imagine is real.

Pablo Picasso, Spanish painter (1881-1973)

A rock pile ceases to be a rock pile the moment a single man contemplates it, bearing with him the image of a cathedral.

Antoine De Saint-Éxupéry, French author (1900-1944)

The man who has no imagination has no wings.

Muhammad Ali, US heavyweight boxing champion (b. 1942)

He who has imagination without learning has wings and no feet.

Joseph Joubert, French essayist, moralist (1754-1824)

Reason can answer questions, but imagination has to ask them.

Ralph Gerard, US psychologist, author

Microsoft's only factory asset is the human imagination.

Bill Gates, US computer engineer, entrepeneur (b. 1955)

What is now proved was once only imagined.

William Blake, British poet, painter, engraver (1757-1827)

Imagination is a quality given a man to compensate him for what he is not, and a sense of humor was provided to console him for what he is.

Oscar Wilde, Irish dramatist, poet (1854-1900)

IMITATION

No man ever yet became great by imitation.

Samuel Johnson, British poet, critic, lexicographer (1709-1784)

When people are free to do as they please, they usually imitate each other.

Eric Hoffer, US philosopher, author, longshoreman (1902-1983)

If you steal from one author, it's plagiarism; if you steal from many, it's research.

Wilson Mizner, US playwright, author (1876-1933)

We forfeit three-fourths of ourselves to be like other people.

Arthur Schopenhauer, German philosopher (1788-1860)

The ideas I stand for are not mine. I borrowed them from Socrates. I swiped them from Chesterfield. I stole them from Jesus. And I put them in a book. If you don't like their rules, whose would you use?

Dale Carnegie, US lecturer, author (1888-1955)

INDIVIDUALITY

Be Daring
Be First
Be Different.

Anita Roddick, British executive, founder of The Body Shop (b. 1943)

Man's main task in life is to give birth to himself, to become what he potentially is. The most important product of his effort is his own personality.

Erich Fromm, US psychologist, philosopher (1900-1980)

The reasonable man adapts himself to the world. The unreasonable man persists in trying to adapt the world to himself. Therefore all progress depends on the unreasonable man.

George Bernard Shaw, Irish playwright, essayist (1856-1950)

Follow the path of the unsafe, independent thinker. Expose your ideas to the dangers of controversy. Speak your mind and fear less the label of 'crackpot' than the stigma of conformity.

Thomas J Watson, US businessman, founder of IBM (1874-1956)

I used to think anyone doing anything weird was weird. Now I know that it is the people that call others weird that are weird.

Sir Paul McCartney, British pop musician (b. 1942)

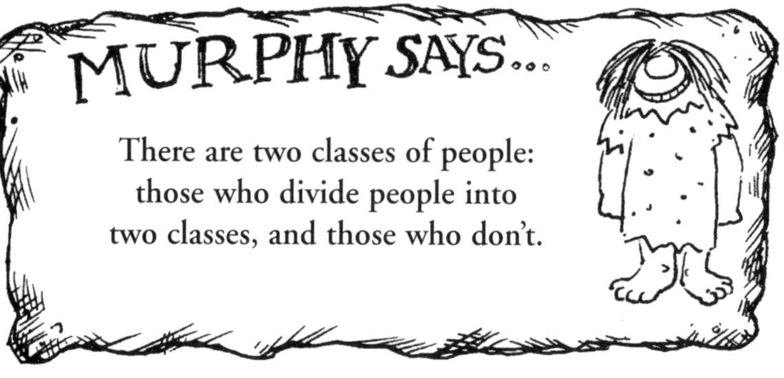

No one can possibly achieve any real and lasting success or get rich in business by being a conformist.

J Paul Getty, US businessman (1892-1976)

Few great players make the transition into management. The reason is that great players are normally like soloists in an orchestra. They perform alone and tend to look down at team-mates with lesser ability.

Bob Paisley, British football manager (1919-1996)

Never play a thing the same way twice.

Louis Armstrong, US jazz musician (1900-1971)

In order to be irreplacable one must always be different.

Coco Chanel, French fashion designer (1883-1971)

You cannot step twice into the same river, for other waters are always flowing on to you.

Heraclitus, Greek philosopher (c535-c475BC)

I can't stand to sing the same song the same way two nights in succession. Let alone two years or ten years. If you can, then it ain't music, it's close-order drill or exercise or yodelling or something, not music.

Billie Holiday, US jazz singer (1915-1959)

INNOVATION

The only sustainable competitive advantage comes from out-innovating the competition.

James Morse, US judge (b. 1940)

Always remember, that someone, somewhere, is making a product that will make your product obsolete.

Georges Doriot, US executive, founder of American R&D (1899-1987)

Once an organisation loses its spirit of pioneering and rests on its early work, its progress stops.

Thomas J Watson, US businessman, founder of IBM (1874-1956)

Don't try to innovate for the future. Innovate for the present.

Peter Drucker, US management author, consultant (b. 1909)

We should do something when people say it is crazy. If people say something is 'good', it means someone else is already doing it.

Hajime Mitarai, Japanese electronics businessman (1938-1995)

In England an inventor is regarded almost as a crazy man, and in too many instances invention ends in disappointment and poverty. In America an inventor is honoured, help is forthcoming, and the exercise of ingenuity, the application of science to the work of man, is there the shortest road to wealth.

Oscar Wilde, Irish dramatist, poet (1854-1900)

Originality is a thing we constantly clamour for, and constantly quarrel with.

Thomas Carlyle, Scottish essayist, historian (1795-1881)

Things don't turn up in this world until somebody turns them up.

James A Garfield, US President (1831-1881)

A new scientific truth does not triumph by convincing its opponents and making them see the light, but rather because its opponents eventually die, and a new generation grows up that is familiar with it.

Max Planck, German physicist (1858-1947)

Invention is the mother of necessity.

Thorstein Veblen, US economist, social scientist (1857-1929)

Why, the greatest invention in history is the safety pin. The second greatest is perforated toilet paper.

Tiny Tim, US entertainer (1932-1996)

My father worked for the same firm for twelve years. They fired him. They replaced him with a tiny gadget this big. It does everything that my father does, only it does it much better. The depressing thing is my mother ran out and bought one.

Woody Allen, US film actor, director (b. 1935)

INTEGRITY

We must adjust to changing times and still hold to unchanging principles.

Jimmy Carter, US President (b. 1924)

Always do right! This will gratify some people and astonish the rest.

Mark Twain, US author (1835-1910)

Resolve to perform what you ought; perform without fail what you resolve.

'Stonewall' Jackson, US general (1842-1863)

So act that your principle of action might safely be made a law for the whole world.

Immanuel Kant, German philosopher (1724-1804)

All ambitions are lawful, except those that climb upward on the miseries or credulities of mankind.

Joseph Conrad, Polish-born British author (1857-1924)

No one can earn a million dollars honestly.

William Jennings Bryan, US statesman (1860-1925)

The measure of a man's real character is what he would do if he knew he would never be found out.

Thomas Babington Macaulay, British historian, essayist (1800-1859)

Character is doing what's right when nobody's looking.

J C Watts, US congressman (b. 1957)

The ultimate measure of a man is not where he stands in moments of comfort, but where he stands at times of challenge and controversy.

Martin Luther King Jr, US civil rights leader (1929-1968)

I either want less corruption, or more chance to participate in it.

Ashleigh Brilliant, British philosopher, author (b. 1933)

It is easier to fight for one's principles than to live up to them.

Alfred Adler, Austrian psychiatrist (1870-1937)

Those are my principles. If you don't like them I have others.

Groucho Marx, US comic actor (1890-1977)

INTERNET

The Internet crosses borders and oceans with daredevil ease. There is no greater challenge to a parochial outlook than a day or two monitoring message traffic in this ongoing worldwide conversation.

Paul Gilster, US science author

E-mail is reincarnating the age of letter writing. We're keeping in touch the way the Victorians did, building a personal community connected by a constant stream of letters sharing news and gossip. E-mail is reviving the 'letter' as a forum for wit, style, and personality, as well as serving as an invaluable business tool.

Leslie Schroeder, US public relations executive

Stop thinking about it as the 'information superhighway' and start thinking about it as the 'marketing superhighway.' Doesn't it sound better already?

Don Logan, US executive, Time Inc

The Internet is a perfect diversion from learning - it opens many doors that lead to empty rooms.

Cliff Stoll, US astronomer (b. 1950)

The Internet is an elite organisation; most of the population of the world has never even made a phone call.

Noam Chomsky, US linguist, political activist (b. 1928)

The greatest asset of this worldwide electronic network, covering millions of individuals and organisations, is the ease with which you can establish a direct relationship with one person.

David Williams, British management author, presenter (b. 1950)

We've all heard that a million monkeys banging on a million typewriters will eventually reproduce the entire works of Shakespeare. Now, thanks to the Internet, we know this is not true.

Eyler Coates, US librarian (b. 1930)

INVOLVEMENT

Tell me and I'll forget.
Teach me and I'll remember.
Involve me and I'll learn.

W Edwards Deming, US statistician, author (1900-1993)

People tend to resist that which is thrust upon them. They tend to support that which they help create.

Vince Pfaff

Retention boils down to basic best practices. A company that engages its people at all levels and in all ways is a company that keeps them.

Barbara Ettorre, US management consultant

Nobody's ever insulted to be invited.

Mrs Leonard Lyons

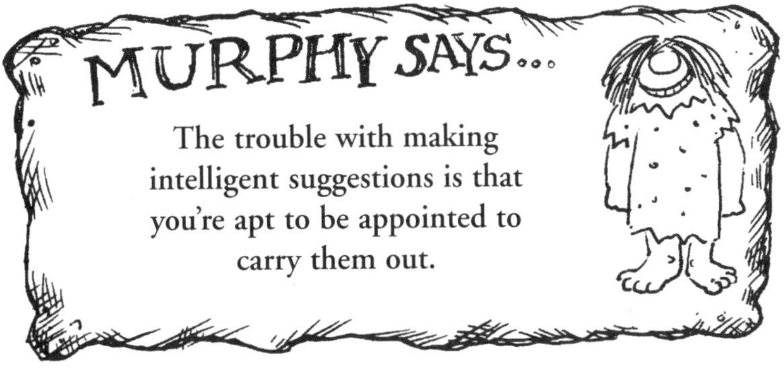

Flow is a state of self-forgetfulness, the opposite of rumination and worry: instead of being lost in nervous pre-occupation, people in flow are so absorbed in the task at hand that they lose all self-consciousness, dropping the small pre-occupations - health, bills, even doing well - of daily life.

Daniel Goleman, US psychologist, author (b. 1946)

Painters must want to paint above all else. If the artist in front of the canvas begins to wonder how much he will sell it for, or what the critics will think of it, he won't be able to pursue original avenues. Creative achievements depend on single-minded immersion.

Mihaly Csikszentmihalyi, US social scientist

JOURNEYS

A journey of a thousand miles starts in front of your feet.

Lao Tzu, Chinese founder of Taoism, author (6th century BC)

None travels so high as he who knows not where he is going.

Oliver Cromwell, English soldier, statesman (1599-1658)

It is good to have an end to journey toward; but it is the journey that matters, in the end.

Ursula K Le Guin, US author (b. 1929)

Do not follow where the path may lead. Go instead where there is no path and leave a trail.

Muriel Strode

If you want to succeed you should strike out on new paths rather than travel the worn paths of accepted status.

John D Rockefeller, US industrialist, philanthropist (1839-1937)

While modelling and matching the styles and processes of others is helpful, remember it's your journey with your own goals, signposts and markers.

Scott Simmerman, US mangement consultant (b. 1948)

Don't worry about genius. Don't worry about being clever. Trust to hard work, perseverance and determination. And the best motto for a long march is: 'Don't grumble. Plug on!'

Margaret Thatcher, British Prime Minister (b. 1925)

I will go anywhere, as long as it be forward.

David Livingstone, Scottish missionary (1813-1873)

Life can only be understood backwards; but it must be lived forward.

Soren Kierkegaard, Danish philosopher (1813-1855)

If everything seems to be coming your way, you're probably in the wrong lane.

We all want progress, but if you're on the wrong road, progress means doing an about-turn and walking back to the right road; in that case, the man who turns back soonest is the most progressive.

C S Lewis, British author, scholar (1898-1963)

There are no shortcuts to any place worth going.

Beverley Sills, US soprano (b. 1929)

Originality is unexplored territory. You get there by carrying a canoe - you can't take a taxi.

Alan Alda, US actor, writer, director (b. 1936)

Throughout the centuries there were men who took first steps down new roads with nothing but their own vision.

Ayn Rand, Russian-born US author (1905-1982)

KNOWLEDGE

To be conscious that you are ignorant is a great step to knowledge.

Benjamin Disraeli, British Prime Minister (1804-1881)

We don't know a millionth of one percent about anything.

Thomas Alva Edison, US inventor (1847-1931)

An investment in knowledge pays the best interest.

Benjamin Franklin, US statesman, author, scientist (1706-1790)

What you don't know will always hurt you.

Throughout history, the craftsman who had learned a trade after five or seven years of apprenticeship had learned, by age eighteen or nineteen, everything he would ever need to use during his lifetime. In the society of organisations, however, it is safe to assume that anyone with any knowledge will have to acquire new knowledge every four or five years or become obsolete.

Peter Drucker, US managment author, consultant (b. 1909)

No amount of sophistication is going to allay the fact that all your knowledge is about the past and all your decisions are about the future.

Ian E Wilson, Canadian cultural administrator (b. 1943)

We are trying to sell more and more intellect, and less and less materials.

George Hegg, Executive, 3M

The factory worker no longer manipulates the sheet of steel; he manipulates the data about the steel.

William Bridges, US engineer, researcher, educator (b. 1934)

The secret of business is to know something that nobody else knows.

Aristotle Onassis, Greek businessman (1906-1975)

The most important part of turnover is the loss of intellectual capital.

Ted Kastelic

If money is your hope for independence you will never have it. The only real security that a man will have in this world is a reserve of knowledge, experience, and ability.

Henry Ford, US automobile manufacturer, engineer (1863-1947)

You never have to know all the answers because you won't be asked all the questions.

Herbert Prochnow, US banker, author (b. 1897)

The more a man knows, the more willing he is to learn. The less a man knows, the more positive he is that he knows everything.

Robert Ingersoll, US lawyer, orator (1833-1899)

To know, is to know that you know nothing. That is the meaning of true knowledge.

Confucius, Chinese philosopher, teacher (551-479 BC)

An expert is one who knows more and more about less and less.

Nicholas Butler, US educator, Nobel Peace Prize winner (1862-1947)

LEADERSHIP

A leader is a dealer in hope.

Napoleon Bonaparte, French soldier, statesman, revolutionary (1769-1821)

Leadership is the transference of vision.

Hal Reed

The key to successful leadership today is influence, not authority.

Kenneth Blanchard, US management author, presenter (b. 1939)

Management is about now, leadership about the future; one implements goals, the other sets them; one relies on control, the other inspires trust; one deals in rational processes, the other in emotional horizons.

Amin Rajan, British economist, researcher, author (b. 1942)

The job of the leader is to speak to the possibility.

Benjamin Zander, British conductor, management presenter (b. 1939)

Good leaders must first become good servants.

Robert Greenleaf, US management consultant, educationist (1904-1990)

A leader takes people where they want to go. A great leader takes people where they don't necessarily want to go but ought to be.

Rosalynn Carter, US first lady (b. 1927)

Managers are often so busy cutting through the undergrowth they don't even realise they are in the wrong jungle. A leader is a person who climbs the tallest tree, surveys the entire situation, and yells, 'Wrong jungle!'

Stephen Covey, US management author, presenter (b. 1932)

People buy into the leader before they buy into the vision.

John C Maxwell, US clergyman, author

I start with the premise that the function of leadership is to produce more leaders, not more followers.

Ralph Nader, US lawyer (b. 1934)

I used to think that running an organisation was equivalent to conducting a symphony orchestra. But I don't think that's quite it; it's more like jazz. There is more improvisation.

Warren Bennis, US academic, management author (b. 1925)

Let me state a basic old form of leadership. This anachronism is the person who in effect says to his organisation, 'I order all of you insignificant little people to come to work excited, energetic, and creative and to accomplish impossible tasks, so that I may become rich and famous and live a luxurious life travelling around the world and building a home on the Riviera and playing golf with other important people like myself. By the way, I want you to park in the outer lot and slog through the snow past the empty parking space with my name on it, and I also want you to pay for your coffee while I get mine free, served on fine china.'

Robert Townsend, US author, businessman (1920-1998)

You manage things; you lead people.

Admiral Grace Murray Hooper, US naval officer, computer programmer (1906-1992)

A leader has a vision and conviction that a dream can be achieved. He inspires the power and energy to get it done.

Ralph Lauren, US fashion designer (b. 1939)

The leader who knows when to listen, when to act, and when to withdraw can work effectively with nearly everyone.

John Heider, US management author

No man is great enough or wise enough for any of us to surrender our destiny to. The only way in which any one can lead us is to restore to us the belief in our own guidance.

Henry Miller, US author (1891-1980)

Mention the word leadership and the vast majority of folks think of Ghandi or Churchill or Iacocca. In doing so, they raise the concept to a level where it seems relevant to a handful of people at most. Thinking that way, the younger manager doesn't try to develop her own leadership potential. Leadership with a small 'l' is of incredible importance in today's world. Needless to say, it would greatly help if we could get more people to think of leadership in the 'small l' sense, and not just the larger than life 'capital L' sense.

John Kotter, US author (b. 1947)

One of the advantages of being a captain is being able to ask for advice without necessarily having to take it.

Captain James T Kirk, character in 'Star Trek'

A leader is best
When people barely know that he exists,
Not so good when people obey and acclaim him,
Worst when they despise him.
'Fail to honour people,
They fail to honour you';
But of a good leader, who talks little,
When his work is done, his aim fulfilled,
They will all say, 'We did this ourselves.'

Lao Tzu, Chinese founder of Taoism, author (6th century BC)

We can't all be heroes because somebody has to sit on the curb and clap as they go by.

Will Rogers, US actor, humorist (1879-1935)

The graveyards are full of indispensable men.

Charles de Gaulle, French President, general (1890-1970)

A politician thinks of the next election - a statesman of the next generation.

James Freeman Clarke, US minister, theologian, writer (1810-1888)

Life is like a dogsled team. If you ain't the lead dog, the scenery never changes.

Lewis Grizzard, US columnist, humorist (1946-1994)

Be willing to make decisions. That's the most important quality in a good leader.

George S Patton, US general (1885-1945)

Eagles don't flock - you have to find them one at a time.

H Ross Perot, US executive, Presidential candidate (b. 1930)

A good leader is a person who takes a little more than his share of the blame and a little less than his share of the credit.

John C Maxwell, US clergyman, author

Make a careful list of all things done to you that you abhorred. Don't do them to others, ever. Make another list of things done to you that you loved. Do them to others, always.

Dee Hock, financial business executive (b. 1930)

LEARNING

I am always doing that which I cannot do, in order that I may learn how to do it.

Pablo Picasso, Spanish painter (1881-1973)

The difference between what the most and the least learned people know is inexpressibly trivial in relation to that which is unknown.

Albert Einstein, German physicist (1879-1955)

At the core of active learning is a deceptively simple requirement; students must be personally invested in the learning process.

David Garvin, US academic, business author

Sit down before a fact as a little child, be prepared to give up every preconceived notion, follow humbly wherever and to whatever abyss nature leads or you shall learn nothing.

T H Huxley, British biologist (1887-1975)

Learn to Unlearn.

R D Laing, British psychiatrist (1927-1989)

Prepare yourself in the subject so well that it shall be always on tap: then in the classroom trust your spontaneity and fling away all further care.

William James, US philosopher, psychologist (1842-1910)

The ability to learn faster than the competition is often the only sustainable competitive advantage a company can have.

Arie de Geus, US oil executive, management author

Over the long run, superior performance depends on superior learning.

Peter Senge, US management author, presenter

The illiterate of the future will not be the person who cannot read. It will be the person who does not know how to learn.

Alvin Toffler, US management author, editor (b. 1928)

In a time of drastic change it is the learners who inherit the future. The learned usually find themselves equipped to live in a world that no longer exists.

Eric Hoffer, US philosopher, author, longshoreman (1902-1983)

I do like challenges. What I like most of all is to learn. When I feel that I've learnt what there is to learn about telecommunications, or airlines, or cosmetics - well, you name it - then I move onto something else.

Richard Branson, British entrepeneur (b. 1950)

The universe is full of magical things patiently waiting for our wits to grow sharper.

Mary Adelaide Eden Philpotts, British author (1896-1996)

I am always ready to learn, but I do not always like being taught.

Winston Churchill, British Prime Minister (1874-1965)

Human beings, who are almost unique in having the ability to learn from the experience of others, are also remarkable for their apparent disinclination to do so.

Douglas Adams, British author (b. 1952)

What did you ask at school today?

Richard Feynman, US physicist, Nobel prize winner, bongo player (1918-1988)

When you read a book, you hold another's mind in your hands.

James Burke, British TV presenter, producer

In the book of life, the answers aren't in the back.

Charlie Brown, cartoon strip character, by Charles Schulz (b. 1922)

LISTENING

We have two ears and one mouth so that we can listen twice as much as we speak.

Epictetus, Greek philosopher (55-135 AD)

The most important thing in communication is to hear what isn't being said.

Peter Drucker, US author, consultant (b. 1909)

If you're talking, you're giving information and therefore giving away power; if you're listening and asking questions, you're gaining information, the raw material of knowledge, and therefore gaining power.

Geoff Burch, British management author, presenter (b. 1951)

One of the best ways to persuade others is with your ears - by listening to them.

Dean Rusk, US statesman (1909-1994)

A good listener is not only popular everywhere, but after a while he gets to know something.

Wilson Mizner, US playwright, author (1876-1933)

It's a mistake to think we listen only with our ears. It's much more important to listen with the mind, the eyes, the body, and the heart. Unless you truly want to understand the other person, you'll never be able to listen.

Mark Herndon, US musician (b. 1955)

MEASUREMENT

Not everything that counts can be counted, and not everything that can be counted, counts.

Sir George Pickering, British clinician (b. 1904)

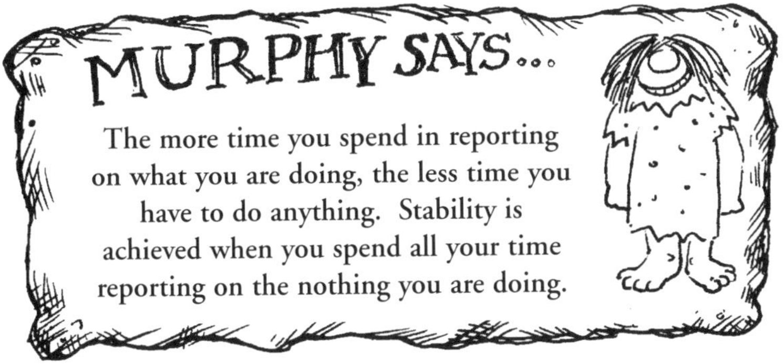

Sometime during the two-year curriculum, every MBA student ought to hear it clearly stated that numbers, techniques and analysis are all side matters. What is central to business is the joy of creating.

Peter Robinson, US executive (b. 1938)

Never measure the height of a mountain until you have reached the top. Then you will see how low it was.

Dag Hammarskjold, Swedish statesman (1905-1961)

What gets measured gets done - but only for the purpose of measurement.

David Williams, British management author, presenter (b. 1950)

MEDIA

A newspaper consists of just the same number of words, whether there be any news or not.

Henry Fielding, British playwright, author (1707-1754)

For most folks, no news is good news; for the press, good news is not news.

Gloria Borger, US journalist

Nothing travels faster than light, with the possible exception of bad news, which follows its own rules.

Douglas Adams, British author (b. 1952)

Newspapers should have no friends.

Joseph Pullitzer, US publisher (1847-1911)

I believe in equality for everyone, except reporters and photographers.

Mahatma Gandhi, Indian nationalist leader (1869-1948)

The camera cannot lie. But it can be an accessory to untruth.

Harold Evans, British journalist (b. 1928)

All photographs are accurate. None of them is the truth.

Richard Avedon, US photographer (b. 1923)

MEDIOCRITY

Some men are born mediocre, some men achieve mediocrity, and some men have mediocrity thrust upon them.

Joseph Heller, US author (b. 1923)

Only the mediocre are always at their best.

Jean Giraudoux, French writer, diplomat (1882-1944)

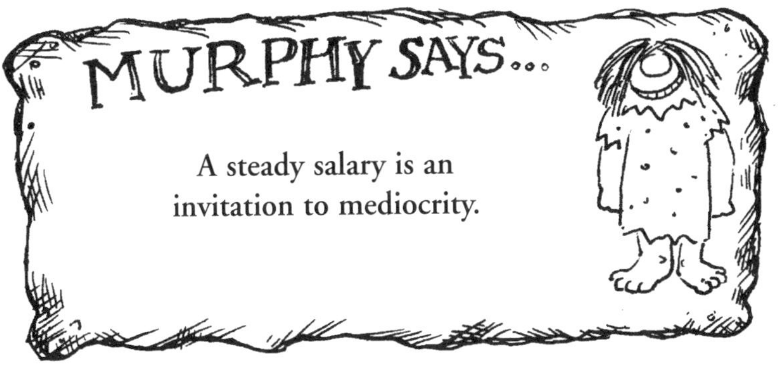

The world is made of people who never quite get into the first team and who just miss the prizes at the flower show.

Jacob Bronowski, British mathematician, scientist (1908-1974)

The mass of men lead lives of quiet desperation and go to the grave with the song still in them.

Henry David Thoreau, US essayist, poet (1817-1862)

MEETINGS

Meetings are indispensable when you don't want to do anything.

John Kenneth Galbraith, US economist, diplomat (b. 1908)

I have noticed that the people who are late are often so much jollier than the people who have to wait for them.

Edward Verrall Lucas, British author, journalist, publisher (1868-1938)

The next time you're in a meeting, look around and identify the yes-butters, the not-knowers, and the why-notters. Why-notters move the world.

Louise Pierson

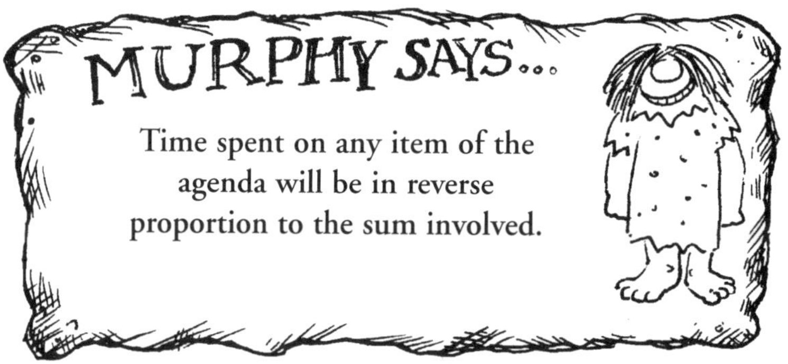

A committee is a cul-de-sac down which ideas are lured and then quietly strangled.

Sir Barnett Cocks, British political author (b. 1907)

Every discussion in a meeting has a diminishing curve of interest. The longer the discussion goes on, the fewer people will be interested in it.

Mark McCormack, US sports agent (b. 1930)

Why do we take notes of meetings that last for hours and call them minutes?

David Williams, British management author, presenter (b. 1950)

A conference is a gathering of important people who singly can do nothing, but together can decide that nothing can be done.

Fred Allen, US supreme court justice (b. 1926)

What is a committee? A group of the unwilling, picked from the unfit, to do the unnecessary.

Richard Harkness, US journalist

MISTAKES

Mistakes are the portals of discovery.

James Joyce, Irish author, poet (1882-1941)

No man ever became great or good except through many and great mistakes.

William Ewart Gladstone, British Prime Minister (1809-1898)

He who never made a mistake never made a discovery.

Samuel Smiles, British author (1812-1904)

Show me a person who has never made a mistake and I'll show you somebody who has never achieved much.

Joan Collins, British actress (b. 1933)

Freedom is not worth having if it does not include the freedom to make mistakes.

Mahatma Gandhi, Indian nationalist leader (1869-1948)

To swear off making mistakes is very easy. All you have to do is swear off having ideas.

Leo Burnett, US advertising executive (1891-1971)

One cannot make an omelette without breaking eggs - but it is amazing how many eggs one can break without making a decent omelette.

Knowledge rests not upon truth alone, but upon error also.

Carl Gustav Jung, Swiss psychiatrist, analytical psychologist (1876-1961)

From error to error one discovers the entire truth.

Sigmund Freud, Austrian founder of psychoanalysis (1856-1939)

Don't 'tolerate' mistakes. Embrace them!

Tom Peters, US management author, presenter (b. 1942)

Experience is simply the name we give our mistakes.

Oscar Wilde, Irish dramatist, poet (1854-1900)

Good judgement comes from experience. Experience comes from bad judgement.

Jim Horning, US computer expert, academic

I have learned throughout my life as a composer chiefly through my mistakes and pursuits of false assumptions, not by my exposure to founts of wisdom and knowledge.

Igor Stravinsky, Russian composer (1882-1971)

A doctor can bury his mistakes but an architect can only advise his clients to plant vines.

Frank Lloyd Wright, US architect (1869-1959)

MOTIVATION

The mind is not a vessel to be filled but a fire to be kindled.

Plutarch, Greek biographer, essayist (46-120 AD)

A key characteristic of transformational leaders is that they motivate people to do more than they originally expected to do.

Elizabeth Chell, British academic, management author (b. 1949)

Martin Luther King did not say
'I have a dream'
to himself.

Benjamin Zander, British conductor, management presenter (b. 1939)

You know, I was stumped one day when a little boy asked, 'Do you draw Mickey Mouse?' I had to admit I do not draw any more. 'Then you think up all the jokes and ideas?' 'No,' I said, 'I don't do that.' Finally, he looked at me and said, 'Mr Disney, just what do you do?' 'Well,' I said, 'Sometimes I think of myself as a little bee. I go from one area of the studio to another and gather pollen and sort of stimulate everybody.' I guess that's the job I do. I certainly don't consider myself a businessman, and I never did believe I was worth anything as an artist.

Walt Disney, US artist, film producer (1901-1966)

Good leadership consists of motivating people to their highest levels by offering them opportunities, not obligations.

John Heider, US management author

Leaders in the new organisation do not lack motivational tools, but the tools are different from those of traditional corporate bureaucrats. The new rewards are based not on status but on contribution, and they consist not of regular promotion and automatic pay rises but of excitement about mission and a share of the glory and the gains of success.

Rosabeth Moss Kanter, US academic, management author (b. 1943)

We don't want satisfaction. We want creative dissatisfaction associated with excitement about the job. That's what motivation is made of.

Daniel Quinn Mills, US academic, management author (b. 1941)

Do you want to sell sugar water all your life, or do you want to come with me and change the world?

Steve Jobs, US executive, co-founder of Apple Computer Inc (b. 1955), persuading John Sculley to leave Pepsi Cola

I'm slowly becoming a convert to the principle that you can't motivate people to do things, you can only demotivate them. The primary job of the manager is not to empower but to remove obstacles.

Scott Adams, US cartoonist, author (b. 1957)

The best motivation is self-motivation. The guy says, 'I wish someone would come by and turn me on.' What if they don't show up? You've got to have a better plan for your life.

Jim Rohn, US motivational speaker, author

Everyone needs to know what is expected of them. Expect people to be better than they are; it helps them to become better. But don't be disappointed when they are not; it helps them to keep trying.

Merry Browne, US poet

The key to motivation is motive.

Roger Merrill, US management consultant, author

In everyone's life, at some time, our inner fire goes out. It is then burst into flames by an encounter with another human being. We should all be thankful for those people who rekindle the inner spirit.

Albert Schweitzer, Alsatian theologian (1875-1965)

I was going to buy a copy of The Power of Positive Thinking, and I thought: What the hell good would that do?

Ronnie Shakes, US humorist

OPPORTUNITY

If opportunity doesn't knock, build a door.

Milton Berle, US actor (b. 1908)

Ability is nothing without opportunity.

Napoleon Bonaparte, French soldier, statesman, revolutionary (1769-1821)

When one door closes, another opens, but we often look so long and regretfully upon the closed door, we do not see the ones which open for us.

Alexander Graham Bell, Scottish inventor (1847-1922)

There is no security on this earth, there is only opportunity.

Douglas MacArthur, US general (1880-1964)

Opportunity is missed by most people because it is dressed in overalls and looks like work.

Thomas Alva Edison, US inventor (1847-1931)

When written in Chinese, the word 'crisis' is composed of two characters. One represents danger and the other represents opportunity.

John F Kennedy, US President (1917-1963)

We are confronted with insurmountable opportunities.

Walt Kelly, US satirist (1913-1973)

The untalented are more at ease in a society that gives them valid alibis for not achieving than in one where opportunities are abundant.

Eric Hoffer, US philosopher, author, longshoreman (1902-1983)

PACE

The first man gets the oyster, the second man gets the shell.

Andrew Carnegie, Scottish industrialist, philanthropist (1835-1919)

Procrastination is the art of keeping up with yesterday.

Donald Marquis, US newspaper owner, poet, playwright (1878-1937)

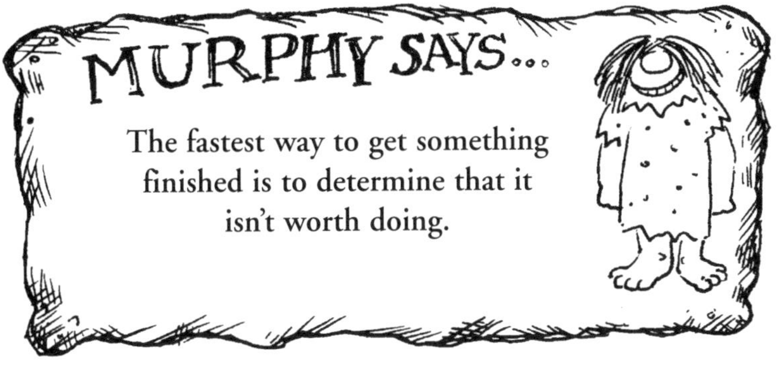

Even if you're on the right track, you'll get run over if you just sit there.

Will Rogers, US actor, humorist (1879-1935)

We live in an age when pizza gets to your home before the police.

Jeff Marder, US humorist, TV presenter

If everything's under control, you're going too slow.

Mario Andretti, Italian racing driver (b. 1940)

The speed of the boss is the speed of the team.

Lee Iacocca, US automotive executive (b. 1924)

There is more to life than increasing its speed.

Mahatma Gandhi, Indian nationalist leader (1869-1948)

The world is moving so fast these days that the man who says it can't be done is generally interrupted by someone doing it.

Harry Emerson Fosdick, US clergyman, author (1878-1969)

PAPERWORK

Report writing, like motor-car driving and love-making, is one of those activities which almost every Englishman thinks he can do well without instruction. The results of course are usually abominable.

Tom Margerison, US photographer

A memorandum is written not to inform the reader but to protect the writer.

Dean Acheson, US statesman, lawyer (1893-1971)

Our customer's paperwork is profit. Our own paperwork is loss.

Unknown accountant

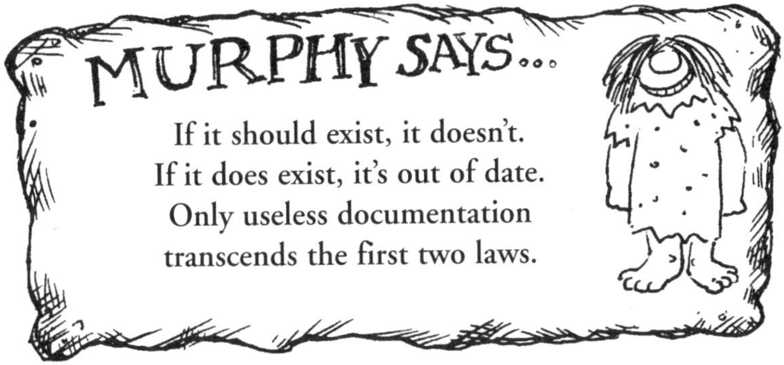

What is written without effort is in general read without pleasure.

Samuel Johnson, British poet, critic, lexicographer (1709-1784)

Writing is easy. All you do is stare at a blank piece of paper until drops of blood form on your forehead.

Gene Fowler, US journalist, biographer (1890-1960)

Having imagination, it takes you an hour to write a paragraph that, if you were unimaginative, would take you only a minute. Or you might not write the paragraph at all.

Franklin P Adams, US journalist, poet, radio personality (1881-1960)

How do I know what I think until I see what I say?

E M Forster, British author (1879-1970)

PASSION

Only passion, great passion, can elevate the human soul to achieve great things.

Denis Diderot, French philosopher (1713-1784)

We may affirm absolutely that nothing great in the world has been accomplished without passion.

Georg Wilhelm Friedrich Hegel, German philosopher (1770-1831)

I don't believe people are looking for the meaning of life as much as they are looking for the experience of being alive.

Joseph Campbell, US author, editor (1904-1987)

One person with a belief is equal to a force of 99 who have only interests.

John Stuart Mill, British philosopher, economist (1806-1873)

Work is love made visible. And if you cannot work with love but only with distaste, it is better that you should leave your work and sit at the gate of the temple and take alms of those who work with joy.

Kahlil Gibran, Lebanese philosopher, author, poet (1883-1931)

Champions aren't made in gyms. Champions are made from something they have deep in them - a desire, a dream, a vision. They have to have the skill, and the will. But the will must be stronger than the skill.

Muhammad Ali, US heavyweight boxing champion (b. 1942)

There is no end. There is no beginning. There is only the infinite passion of life.

Federico Fellini, Italian film director (b. 1920)

PLANNING

If you are leaping a ravine, the moment of takeoff is a bad time for considering alternative strategies.

John Cleese, British actor, author (b. 1939)

Men never plan to be failures; they simply fail to plan to be successful.

William A Ward, British diplomat (b. 1928)

Plans are useless, but planning is essential.

Dwight D Eisenhower, US President, general (1890-1969)

Nothing is particularly hard if you divide it into small jobs.

Henry Ford, US automobile manufacturer, engineer (1863-1947)

Chance favours only the prepared mind.

Louis Pasteur, French chemist, microbiologist (1822-1895)

Organisation can never be a substitute for initiative and judgement.

Louis Brandeis, US supreme court justice (1856-1941)

Life is what happens to you while you're busy making other plans.

John Lennon, British pop musician (1940-1980)

POSSIBILITY

Treat a man as he is and he will remain as he is. Treat a man as he can and should be and he will become as he can and should be.

Johann Wolfgang von Goethe, German poet, letter-writer (1749-1832)

There is no person living who isn't capable of doing more than he thinks he can do.

Henry Ford, US automobile manufacturer, engineer (1863-1947)

First say to yourself what you would be; and then do what you have to do.

Epictetus, Greek philosopher (55-135 AD)

I only speak to the 'A' in people and I set as the goal the maximum capacity that people have. I settle for no less. I make myself a relentless architect of the possibilities of human beings.

Benjamin Zander, British conductor, management presenter (b. 1939)

To find in ourselves what makes life worth living is a risky business, for it means that once we know we must seek it. It also means that without it life will be valueless.

Marsha Sinetar, US management author

It is difficult to say what is impossible, for the dream of yesterday is the hope of today and the reality of tomorrow.

Bob Goddard, US physicist, rocketry pioneer (1882-1945)

You wake up in the morning, and your purse is magically filled with twenty-four hours of unmanufactured tissue of the universe of life! It is yours. It is the most precious of possessions. No one can take it from you. And no one receives either more or less than you receive.

Arnold Bennett, British novelist (1867-1931)

I am inclined by nature to be optimistic about the capacity of a person to rise higher than he or she has thought possible once interest and ambition are aroused.

Dwight D Eisenhower, US President, general (1890-1969)

Things are only impossible until they're not.

Captain Jean-Luc Picard, character in 'Star Trek: The Next Generation'

If an elderly but distinguished scientist says that something is possible he is almost certainly right, but if he says that it is impossible he is very probably wrong.

Arthur C Clarke, British author (b. 1917)

What lies behind us and what lies before us are small matters compared to what lies within us.

Ralph Waldo Emerson, American essayist, poet (1803-1882)

Of course we all have our limits, but how can you possibly find your boundaries unless you explore as far and as wide as you possibly can? I would rather fail in an attempt at something new and uncharted than safely succeed in a repeat of something I have done.

Aaron E Hotchner, US author (b. 1920)

If someone says 'can't,' that shows you what to do.

John Cage, US composer (b. 1912)

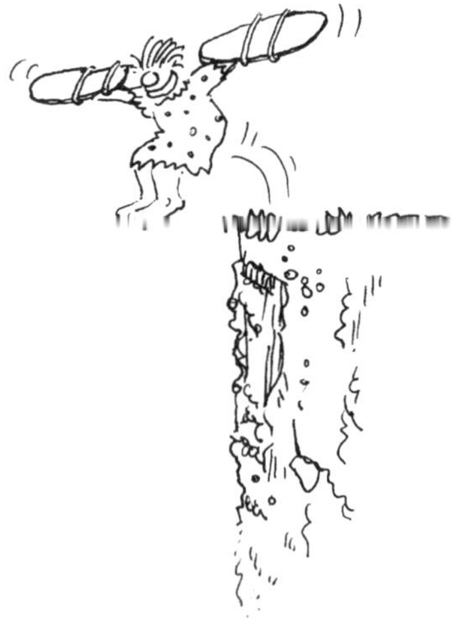

Anything is possible if you don't know what you're talking about.

Nothing splendid has ever been achieved except by those who dared believe that something inside of them was superior to circumstance.

Bruce Barton, US author, advertising executive (1886-1967)

POWER

Being in power is like being a lady. If you have to tell people you are, you aren't.

Margaret Thatcher, British Prime Minister (b. 1925)

Nearly all men can stand adversity, but if you want to test a man's character, give him power.

Abraham Lincoln, US President (1809-1865)

It's not a question of how much power you can hoard for yourself, but how much you can give away.

Benjamin Zander, British conductor, management presenter (b. 1939)

He who has great power should use it lightly.

Seneca, Roman philosopher, statesman, author (3 BC-65 AD)

Never underestimate the power of the powerless.

David Williams, British management author, presenter (b. 1950)

PREDICTIONS

Prediction is extremely difficult. Especially about the future.

Niels Bohr, Danish physicist (b. 1922)

Inventions have long since reached their limit, and I see no hope for further development.

Julius Sextus Frontinus, Roman engineer (1st century AD)

Everything that can be invented has been invented.

Charles Duell, US director of Patents Office (1899)

What sir, would you make a ship sail against the wind and currents by lighting a bonfire under her deck? I pray you excuse me. I have no time to listen to such nonsense.

Napoleon Bonaparte, French soldier, statesman, revolutionary (1769-1821)

Rail travel at high speed is not possible because passengers, unable to breathe, would die of asphyxia.

Dionysius Lardner, British scientist (1793-1859)

This 'telephone' has too many shortcomings to be seriously considered as a means of communication. The device is inherently of no value to us.

Western Union internal memo (1876)

The Americans have need of the telephone, but we do not. We have plenty of messenger boys.

Sir William Preece, Welsh chief engineer of the British Post Office (1834-1913)

Heavier-than-air flying machines are impossible.

Lord Kelvin, Scottish physicist (1824-1907)

While theoretically and technically television may be feasible, commercially and financially I consider it an impossibility, a development of which we need waste little time dreaming.

Lee DeForest, US inventor (1873-1961)

We must not be misled to our own detriment to assume that the untried machine can displace the proved and tried horse.

John K Herr, US general (1878-1955)

There is no likelihood man can ever tap the power of the atom.

Robert Millikan, US physicist, Nobel prize winner (1868-1953)

Who the hell wants to hear actors talk?

H M Warner, Polish/US Hollywood producer (1881-1958)

The talking picture will not supplant the regular silent motion picture.

Thomas Alva Edison, US inventor (1847-1931)

The phonograph is not of any commercial value.

Thomas Alva Edison, US inventor (1847-1931)

I think there is a world market for maybe five computers.

Thomas J Watson, US businessman, founder of IBM (1874-1956)

Computers in the future may weigh no more than 1.5 tons.

Popular Mechanics, forecasting the relentless march of science (1949)

It would appear that we have reached the limits of what it is possible to achieve with computer technology, although one should be careful with such statements, as they tend to sound pretty silly in 5 years.

John Von Neumann, US mathematician (1903-1957)

There is no reason for any individual to have a computer in his home.

Ken Olson, US executive, President of Digital Equipment (b. 1926)

We don't like their sound, and guitar music is on the way out.

Decca Recording Company, rejecting the Beatles (1962)

The concept is interesting and well-informed, but in order to earn better than a 'C', the idea must be feasible.

Yale University management professor in response to Fred Smith's paper proposing reliable overnight delivery service

(Smith went on to found Federal Express)

So we went to Atari and said, 'Hey we've got this amazing thing, even built some of the parts, and what do you think about funding us? Or we'll give it to you. We just want to do it. Pay our salary, we'll come work for you.' And they said, 'No' So then we went to Hewlett-Packard, and they said. 'Hey we don't need you. You haven't got through college yet.'

Steve Jobs, US executive, co-founder of Apple Computer Inc (b. 1955)

PRESENTATION

It usually takes more than three weeks to prepare a good impromptu speech.

Mark Twain, US author (1835-1910)

I can never remember being afraid of an audience. If the audience could do better, they'd be up here on stage and I'd be out there watching them.

Ethel Merman, US singer, actress (1909-1984)

It's all right to have butterflies in your stomach. Just get them to fly in formation.

Rob Gilbert, Australian academic, sociologist

If I went back to college again, I'd concentrate on two areas: learning to write and to speak before an audience. Nothing in life is more important than the ability to communicate effectively.

Gerald Ford, US President (b. 1913)

No one can say just how long a message should be, but you rarely hear complaints about a speech being too short. The amateur worries about what he is going to put in his speech. The expert worries about what he should take out. An artistic performance is concentrated, has a central focus.

Edgar Dale, US media guru

PROBLEMS

There is no such thing as a problem without a gift for you in its hand.

Richard Bach, US author (b. 1936)

There is only one way to happiness and that is to cease worrying about things which are beyond the power of our will.

Epictetus, Greek philosopher (55-135 AD)

There are two kinds of worries - those you can do something about and those you can't. Don't spend any time on the latter.

Duke Ellington, US composer, arranger, pianist (1899-1974)

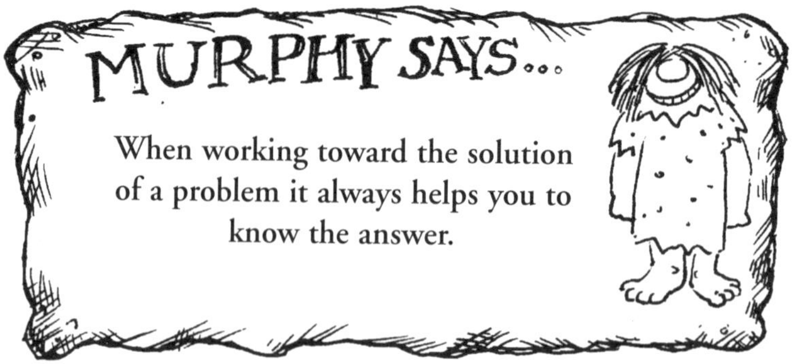

Golf without bunkers and hazards would be tame and monotonous. So would life.

B C Forbes, Scottish journalist (1880-1954)

A problem well stated is a problem half solved.

Charles Kettering, US engineer, inventor (1876-1958)

If the only tool you have is a hammer, you tend to see every problem as a nail.

Abraham Maslow, US psychologist, philosopher (1908-1970)

A man of character finds a special attractiveness in difficulty, since it is only by coming to grips with difficulty that he can realise his potentialities.

Charles de Gaulle, French President, general (1890-1970)

Obstacles are things a person sees when he takes his eyes off his goal.

E Joseph Cossman, US entrepreneur, sales author

PROFITS

The worst crime against working people is a company which fails to operate at a profit.

Samuel Gompers, British politician (1850-1924)

Whoever could make two ears of corn or two blades of grass to grow upon a spot of ground where only one grew before would deserve better of mankind and do more essential service to his country than the whole race of politicians put together.

Jonathan Swift, Irish clergyman, poet, satirist (1667-1745)

Watch the costs and the profits will take care of themselves.

Andrew Carnegie, Scottish industrialist, philanthropist (1835-1919)

The most important thing in life is not simply to capitalise on your gains. Any fool can do that. The important thing is to profit from your losses. That requires intelligence, and makes the difference between a man of sense and a fool.

Dale Carnegie, US lecturer, author (1888-1955)

I had no ambition to make a fortune. Mere money-making has never been my goal, I had an ambition to build.

John D Rockefeller, US industrialist, philanthropist (1839-1937)

A business that makes nothing but money is a poor kind of business.

Henry Ford, US automobile manufacturer, engineer (1863-1947)

Always concentrate on the service or product you provide first and the financial rewards second. Money is a byproduct of excellence. Always make 'doing what is right' your main priority and the financial rewards will follow.

Larry Harmon, US entertainer, aka *Bozo the Clown*

Money often costs too much.

Ralph Waldo Emerson, American essayist, poet (1803-1882)

Surplus wealth is a sacred trust which its possessor is bound to administer in his lifetime for the good of the community.

Andrew Carnegie, Scottish industrialist, philanthropist (1835-1919)

Never get so busy making a living that you forget to make a life.

Paula

PUBLIC RELATIONS

Some are born great, some achieve greatness, and some hire public relations officers.

Daniel J Boorstin, US media author, historian (b. 1914)

Nobody believes the official spokesman - but everyone trusts an unidentified source.

Ron Nesen, US government press officer

An issue ignored is a crisis ensured.

Henry Kissinger, German-born US diplomat, political scientist (b. 1923)

News and political broadcasting bores its audience off the air as soon as it slides from controversy into public relations.

Paul Foot, British journalist

QUALITY

It's a funny thing about life; if you refuse to accept anything but the best, you very often get it.

Somerset Maugham, British author, dramatist (1874-1965)

Find the qualities in your people and you find the quality in your company.

Sir Simon Hornby, British businessman

How long does it take you, as a boss, to achieve world-class quality? Less than a nanosecond to attain it, a lifetime of passionate pursuit to maintain it.

Tom Peters, US management author, presenter (b. 1942)

Quality is free.

Phil Crosby, US consultant, author (b. 1926)

In communities where men build ships for their own sons to fish or fight from, quality is never a problem.

J Deville

With ISO 9000 you can still have terrible processes and products. You can certify a manufacturer that makes life jackets from concrete, as long as those jackets are made according to the documented procedures and the company provides the next of kin with instructions on how to complain about defects.

Richard Buetow, US executive, Motorola

Don't confuse consistency with quality. The customer decides what quality is by their own standards.

Geoff Burch, British management author, presenter (b. 1951)

Consistency is the last refuge of the unimaginative.

Oscar Wilde, Irish dramatist, poet (1854-1900)

The trouble with doing something right the first time is that nobody appreciates how difficult it was.

Walt West

It is a very sobering feeling to be up in space and realise that one's safety factor was determined by the lowest bidder on a government contract.

Alan Shephard, US astronaut (b. 1923)

The greater the emphasis on perfection the further it recedes.

Haridas Chaudhuri, Indian philosopher, author

Quality Control starts and ends with training.

Kaoru Ishikawa, Japanese quality guru, author (b. 1915)

The CEO of a small company decided they needed a motto to commemorate their longevity in the industry. This is what he came up with: 'Our innovation makes us first - our quality makes us last!'

Scott Adams, US cartoonist, author (b. 1957)

QUESTIONS

There are no foolish questions and no man becomes a fool until he has stopped asking questions.

Charles Steinmetz, US electrical engineer (1865-1923)

He who asks is a fool for five minutes, but he who does not ask remains a fool forever.

Chinese proverb

The wise man doesn't give us the right answers, he poses the right questions.

Claude Levi-Strauss, French anthropologist (b. 1908)

Judge a man by his questions rather than by his answers.

Voltaire, French philosopher (1694-1778)

Millions saw the apple fall but Newton was the one to ask why.

Bernard Baruch, US statesman, businessman (1870-1965)

That is the essence of science: ask an impertinent question, and you are on the way to a pertinent answer.

Jacob Bronowski, British mathematician, scientist (1908-1974)

I keep six honest serving men (they taught me all I knew): their names are What and Why and When and How and Where and Who.

Rudyard Kipling, British author, poet (1865-1936)

If you don't ask 'why this?' often enough, somebody will ask 'why you?'.

Tom Hirshfield, US IT author

RECOGNITION

That little packet of responsibility (job description), rewarded in accordance with a fixed formula (pay level), and a single reporting relationship (place in the chain of command) is a roadblock on the highway of change.

William Bridges, US engineer, researcher, educator (b. 1934)

We have to switch incentives from careers, level and promotion, to personal reputation, teamwork and challenging assignments. People then need to feel they can influence, rather than just be rewarded by promotion.

Rosabeth Moss Kanter, US academic, management author (b. 1943)

The difference between a lady and a flower girl is not how she behaves but how she is treated. I shall always be a flower girl to Professor Higgins because he always treats me as a flower girl and always will; but I know I can be a lady to you because you always treat me as a lady and always will.

Eliza Doolittle, character in 'Pygmalion' by George Bernard Shaw (1856-1950)

People who work sitting down get paid more than people who work standing up.

Ogden Nash, US humorous writer (1902-1971)

REFLECTION

To do great work, a man must be very idle as well as very industrious.

Samuel Butler, British author (1835-1902)

Conversation enriches the understanding, but solitude is the school of genius.

Edward Gibbon, British historian (1737-1794)

Some days you must learn a great deal, but you should also have days when you allow what is already in you to swell up and touch everything. If you never let that happen, then you just accumulate facts, and they begin to rattle around inside of you.

E L Konigsburg, US author (b. 1930)

Sit in reverie and watch the changing colour of the waves that break upon the idle seashore of the mind.

Henry Wadsworth Longfellow, US poet (1807-1882)

It is generally recognised that creativity requires leisure, an absence of rush, time for the mind and imagination to float and wander and roam, time for the individual to descend into the depths of his or her psyche, to be available to barely audible signals rustling for attention. Long periods of time may pass in which nothing seems to be happening. But we know that kind of space must be created if the mind is to leap out of its accustomed ruts, to part from the standard, and generate a leap into the new.

Nathaniel Branden, US psychologist, author

If you happen to be one of the fretful minority who can do creative work, never force an idea; you'll abort it if you do. Be patient and you'll give birth to it when the time is ripe. Learn to wait.

Robert Heinlein, US author (1907-1988)

Allow regular time for silent reflection. Turn inward and digest what has happened. Let the senses rest and grow still.

John Heider, US management author

Before I compose a piece, I walk around it several times, accompanied by myself.

Erik Satie, French composer (1866-1925)

Solitude is as needful to the imagination as society is wholesome for the character.

James Russell Lowell, US poet, critic, statesman (1819-1891)

You must learn to be still in the midst of activity and to be vibrantly alive in repose.

Indira Gandhi, Indian Prime Minister (1917-1984)

It would do the world good if every man would compel himself occasionally to be absolutely alone. Most of the world's progress has come out of such loneliness.

Bruce Barton, US author, advertising executive (1886-1967)

Silence is the element in which great things fashion themselves together, that at length they may emerge, full-formed and majestic, into the daylight of life.

Kahlil Gibran, Lebanese philosopher, author, poet (1883-1931)

Don't just do it, stand there!

David Williams, British management author, presenter (b. 1950)

Your vision will become clear only when you look into your heart. Who looks outside, dreams. Who looks inside, awakens.

Carl Gustav Jung, Swiss psychiatrist, analytical psychologist (1876-1961)

RELATIONSHIPS

Don't walk in front of me, I may not follow.
Don't walk behind me, I may not lead.
Just walk beside me, and be my friend.

Albert Camus, French/Algerian existentialist author (1913-1960)

Leadership is Relationship.

Benjamin Zander, British conductor, management presenter (b. 1939)

You can't shake hands with a clenched fist.

Indira Gandhi, Indian Prime Minister (1917-1984)

There is a subterranean emotional economy that passes amongst us all. In every interaction we can make people feel better or worse.

Daniel Goleman, US psychologist, author (b. 1946)

A wise man knows everything; a shrewd one everybody.

Fortune Cookie

If you approach each new person you meet in a spirit of adventure, you will find yourself endlessly fascinated by the new channels of thought and experience and personality that you encounter. I do not mean simply the famous people of the world, but people from every walk and condition of life.

Eleanor Roosevelt, US United Nations delegate (1884-1962)

RESISTANCE

If you want to make enemies, try to change something.

Woodrow Wilson, US President (1856-1924)

People are very open minded about new things - as long as they're exactly like the old ones.

Charles Kettering, US engineer, inventor (1876-1958)

It must be remembered that there is nothing more difficult to plan, more doubtful of success, nor more dangerous to manage, than the creation of a new system. For the initiator has the enmity of all who would profit by the preservation of the old institutions and merely lukewarm defenders in those who would gain by the new ones.

Niccolo Machiavelli, Italian political theorist (1469-1527)

The soft-minded man always fears change. He feels security in the status quo, and he has an almost morbid fear of the new. For him, the greatest pain is the pain of a new idea.

Martin Luther King Jr, US civil rights leader (1929-1968)

Men often oppose a thing merely because they have had no agency in planning it, or because it may have been planned by those whom they dislike.

Alexander Hamilton, US statesman (1757-1804)

Every advance in civilization has been denounced while it was still recent.

Bertrand Russell, British philosopher, mathematician (1872-1970)

He who is firmly seated in authority soon learns to think security, and not progress, the highest lesson of statecraft.

James Russell Lowell, US poet, critic, statesman (1819-1891)

If I have not seen as far as others, it is because giants were standing on my shoulders.

Hal Abelson, US computer academic, author

He who rejects change is the architect of decay. The only human institution which rejects progress is in the cemetery.

Harold Wilson, British Prime Minister (1916-1995)

It is not necessary to change. Survival is not mandatory.

W Edwards Deming, US statistician, author (1900-1993)

The sad fact is that organisations change as little as they can rather than as much as they should.

Barry A Stein, US management author, consultant

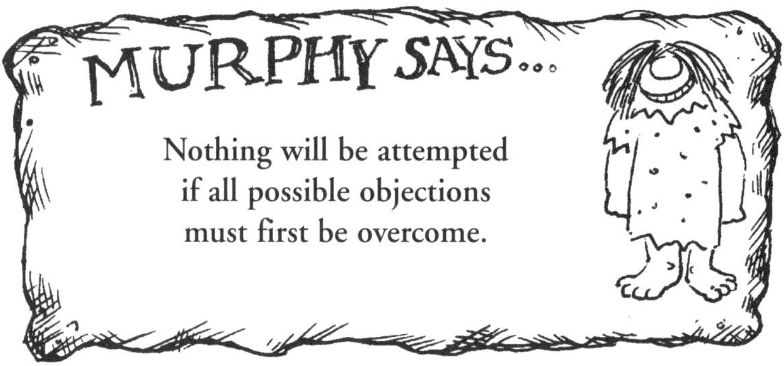

Change is always a threat when done to people, but it's embraced as an opportunity when it is done by people.

Rosabeth Moss Kanter, US academic, management author (b. 1943)

You can't wake a person who is pretending to be asleep.

Navajo proverb

The human mind treats a new idea the same way the body treats a strange protein; it rejects it.

Peter Medawar, Brazilian-born British biologist (1915-1987)

Opposition brings concord. Out of discord comes the greatest harmony.

Heraclitus of Ephesus, Greek philosopher, (535-475 BC)

RISK

The desire for safety stands against every great and noble enterprise.

Cornelius Tacitus, Roman historian (55-120 AD)

People wish to learn to swim and at the same time to keep one foot on the ground.

Marcel Proust, French author (1871-1922)

A ship in harbour is safe,
but that is not what ships are built for.

William Shedd, US author, moralist

People cannot discover new oceans
until they lose sight of the shore.

André Gide, French novelist, critic (1869-1951)

Don't play for safety - it's the most dangerous thing in the world.

Horace Walpole, British author (1717-1797)

And the trouble is, if you don't risk anything, you risk even more.

Erica Jong, US author, poet (b. 1942)

Safe is risky.

Gene Pressman, US clothing retailer

To win without risk is to triumph without glory.

Pierre Corneille, French playwright (1606-1684)

It is the business of the future to be dangerous.

Alfred North Whitehead, British philosopher, mathematician (1861-1947)

If the odds are a million to one against something occurring, chances are 50-50 it will.

What would you attempt to do if you knew you could not fail?

Robert Schuller, US clergyman, author (b. 1926)

There is always a certain risk in being alive, and if you are more alive there is more risk.

Henrick Ibsen, Norwegian playwright, poet (1828-1906)

If you play safe in life, you've decided that you don't want to grow any more.

Shirley Hufstedler, US lawyer, federal judge (b. 1925)

Be daring, be different, be impractical; be anything that will assert integrity of purpose and imaginative vision against the play-it-safers, the creatures of the commonplace, the slaves of the ordinary.

Sir Cecil Beaton, British photographer (1904-1980)

There are risks and costs to a programme of action, but they are far less than the long-range risks and costs of comfortable inaction.

John F Kennedy, US President (1917-1963)

A banker is a fellow who lends you his umbrella when the sun is shining, but wants it back the minute it begins to rain.

Mark Twain, US author (1835-1910)

A bank is a place that will lend you money if you can prove that you don't need it.

Bob Hope, US comedian (b. 1903)

ROLE MODELS

Lives of great men all remind us
We can make our lives sublime,
And, departing, leave behind us
Footprints on the sands of time.

Henry Wadsworth Longfellow, US poet (1807-1882)

Leaders get out in front and stay there by raising the standards by which they judge themselves - and by which they are willing to be judged.

Fredrick Smith, British politician (1872-1930)

The core leadership strategy is simple: be a model. Commit yourself to your own personal mastery. Talking about personal mastery may open people's minds somewhat, but actions always speak louder than words. There's nothing more powerful you can do to encourage others in their quest for personal mastery than to be serious in your own quest.

Peter Senge, US management author, presenter

Become a role model. Like a good doctor, keep learning. Demonstrate that you are a synthesiser, or better yet a humaniser, rather than merely an analyser or energiser by participating in the interactive dialogue and defining part of your work as the development of people and teams.

Michael Maccoby, US management author, psychologist (b. 1933)

If I am walking with two other men, each of them will serve as my teacher. I will pick out the good points of the one and imitate them, and the bad points of the other and correct them in myself.

Confucius, Chinese philosopher, teacher (551-479 BC)

Excellence is a better teacher than mediocrity. The lessons of the ordinary are everywhere. Truly profound and original insights are to be found only in studying the exemplary.

Warren Bennis, US academic, management author (b. 1925)

People have more need for models than for critics.

Scott Simmerman, US mangement consultant (b. 1948)

Few things are harder to put up with than the annoyance of a good example.

Mark Twain, US author (1835-1910)

RULES

Hell, there are no rules here - we're trying to accomplish something.

Thomas Alva Edison, US inventor (1847-1931)

Rule No. 6:
Don't take yourself so goddam' seriously.
There are no other rules.

Benjamin Zander, British conductor, management presenter (b. 1939)

The fun isn't in the rules, it's in the doing.

David Firth, British management author (b. 1949)

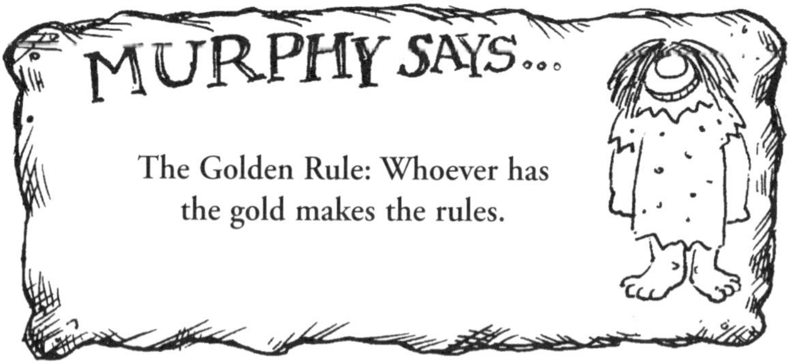

The golden rule is that there are no golden rules.

George Bernard Shaw, Irish playwright, essayist (1856-1950)

SELF-CONFIDENCE

For a man to achieve all that is demanded of him he must regard himself as greater than he is.

Johann Wolfgang von Goethe, German poet, letter-writer (1749-1832)

And above all things, never think that you're not good enough yourself. A man should never think that. My belief is that in life people will take you at your own reckoning.

Anthony Trollope, British author (1815-1882)

No one can make you feel inferior without your consent.

Eleanor Roosevelt, US United Nations delegate (1884-1962)

If you are always worried about how you are performing a task, about how others perceive your performance, you will never perform it well. Performance requires forgetting yourself.

Richard Saul Wurman, US architect, author (b. 1935)

The battles that count aren't the ones for gold medals. The struggles within yourself - the invisible, inevitable battles inside all of us - that's where it's at.

Jesse Owens, US athlete (1913-1980)

When we examine our self-image we tend to find that it has been formulated by the information we have been given by others about ourselves; the art teacher who continually tells us we will never be a painter; the parent who tells us every day that we are too soft and sensitive; the bully who is praised by his bully father; and so on.

Trevor Bentley, US facilitator, author

Our deepest fear is not that we are inadequate. Our deepest fear is that we are powerful beyond measure. It is our light, not our darkness, that most frightens us. We ask ourselves, 'Who am I to be brilliant, gorgeous, talented and fabulous?' Actually, who are you not to be? You are a child of God. Your playing small doesn't serve the world. There's nothing enlightened about shrinking so that other people won't feel insecure around you. We were born to make manifest the glory of God that is within us. It's not just in some of us; it's in everyone. And as we let our own light shine, we unconsciously give other people permission to do the same. As we are liberated from our own fear, our presence automatically liberates others.

Nelson Mandela, South African statesman (b. 1918)

Getting ahead in a difficult profession requires avid faith in yourself. That is why some people with mediocre talent, but with great inner drive, go much further than people with vastly superior talent.

Sophia Loren, Italian actress (b. 1934)

The real 'haves' are they who can acquire freedom, self-confidence, and even riches without depriving others of them. They acquire all of these by developing and applying their potentialities. On the other hand, the real 'have nots' are they who cannot have aught except by depriving others of it. They can feel free only by diminishing the freedom of others, self-confident by spreading fear and dependence among others, and rich by making others poor.

Eric Hoffer, US philosopher, author, longshoreman (1902-1983)

An individual's self-concept is the core of his personality. It affects every aspect of human behaviour: the ability to learn, the capacity to grow and change. A strong, positive self-image is the best possible preparation for success in life.

Joyce Brothers, US TV personality, psychologist (b. 1949)

Confidence is believing you have something to teach; arrogance is the belief you have nothing to learn.

Dale Dauten, US newspaper columnist, (b. 1950)

There are two types of people - those who come into a room and say, 'Well, here I am!' and those who come in and say, 'Ah, there you are.'

Frederick L Collins

I can say, 'I am terribly frightened and fear is terrible and awful and it makes me uncomfortable, so I won't do that because it's uncomfortable. Or I could say 'Get used to being uncomfortable.' It is uncomfortable doing something that's risky. But so what? Do you want to stagnate and just be comfortable?

Barbra Streisand, US singer, actress (b. 1942)

Be thine own palace, or the world's thy jail.

John Donne, British poet (1572-1631)

Self-confidence is the first requisite to great undertakings.

Samuel Johnson, British poet, critic, lexicographer (1709-1784)

SELLING

If you want to buy from us we speak English, but if you want to sell to us you must speak German.

Helmut Kohl, German statesman (b. 1930)

The merchant has no country.

Thomas Jefferson, US President (1741-1826)

Production minus sales equals scrap.

John Fenton, British sales author, presenter

When we sell products, we don't sell objects, we sell feelings.

Geoff Burch, British management author, presenter (b. 1951)

It's not creative unless it sells.

David Ogilvy, US advertising executive, author (b. 1911)

Plan the sale when you plan the ad.

Leo Burnett, US advertising executive (1891-1971)

Don't say yes until I finish talking.

Darryl F Zanuck, US film producer, script writer (1902-1979)

Consultants don't come to your business to give you advice - they come to raise an invoice.

Alan Sugar, British entrepeneur, Amstrad (b. 1947)

You can't stay in your corner of the forest waiting for others to come to you. You have to go to them sometimes.

Winnie the Pooh, character in a book by A.A. Milne (1882-1956)

Life is pain. Anyone who says differently is selling something.

Westley in the film 'The Princess Bride'

SIZE

Hey, size works against excellence.

Bill Gates, US computer engineer, entrepeneur (b. 1955)

Size isn't everything. The whale is endangered, while the ant continues to do just fine.

Bill Vaughan, US journalist, author (1915-1977)

If you think you're too small to have an impact, try going to bed with a mosquito in the room.

Anita Roddick, British executive, founder of The Body Shop (b. 1943)

Any intelligent fool can make things bigger, more complex, and more violent. It takes a touch of genius - and a lot of courage - to move in the opposite direction.

E F Schumacher, German-born British economist (1911-1977)

What we are doing is just a drop in the ocean. But if that drop was not in the ocean, I think the ocean would be less because of that missing drop. I do not agree with the big way of doing things.

Mother Teresa, Albanian charity worker (1910-1997)

It's a small world, but I wouldn't want to paint it.

Steven Wright, Canadian comedian (b. 1955)

SUCCESS

Secrets for success:

1 Get up early
2 Work hard
3 Find oil

J Paul Getty, US businessman (1892-1976)

Here is the prime condition of success: having begun one line, resolve to fight it out on that line, to lead in it, adopt every improvement, have the best machinery, and know the most about it.

Andrew Carnegie, Scottish industrialist, philanthropist (1835-1919)

Success is a great deodorant

Elizabeth Taylor, British-born US actress (b. 1932)

Glory is fleeting, but obscurity is forever.

Napoleon Bonaparte, French soldier, statesman, revolutionary (1769-1821)

Most successes are unhappy. That's why they are successes - they have to reassure themselves about themselves by achieving something that the world will notice.

Agatha Christie, British author (1890-1976)

Success is not the key to happiness. Happiness is the key to success. If you love what you are doing, you will be successful.

Herman Cain, US food executive (b. 1948)

Success in highest and noblest form calls for peace of mind and enjoyment and happiness which comes only to the man who has found the work he likes best.

Napoleon Hill, US motivational author, lecturer (1883-1970)

The fact remains that the overwhelming majority of people who have become wealthy have become so thanks to work they found profoundly absorbing. The long term study of people who eventually became wealthy clearly reveals that their 'luck' arose from accidental dedication they had to an area they enjoyed.

Srully Blotnick, US business author

We must believe in luck. For how else can we explain the success of those we don't like?

Jean Cocteau, French poet, playwright, film director (1889-1963)

Everybody loves success, but they hate successful people.

John McEnroe, US tennis player (b. 1959)

It is not enough to succeed. Others must fail.

Gore Vidal, US author, essayist (b. 1925)

Eighty percent of success is showing up.

Woody Allen, US film actor, director (b. 1935)

I always wanted to be somebody, but I should have been more specific.

Lily Tomlin, US comic actress (b. 1939)

Success seems to be connected with action. Successful people keep moving. They make mistakes, but they don't quit.

Conrad Hilton, US businessman, founder of Hilton Hotels (1887-1979)

Nothing recedes like success.

Walter Winchell, US journalist, broadcaster (1897-1972)

If everything seems to be going well, you have obviously overlooked something.

Success is a state of mind. If you want success, start thinking of yourself as a success.

Joyce Brothers, US TV personality, psychologist (b. 1949)

To know how to wait is the great secret of success.

Joseph Marie De Maistre, French diplomat, writer (1753-1821)

TEAMWORK

Coming together is a beginning. Keeping together is progress. Working together is success.

Henry Ford, US automobile manufacturer, engineer (1863-1947)

Upon the conduct of each depends the fate of all.

Alexander the Great, King of Macedon (356-323 BC)

When a blind man carries a lame man, both go forward.

Josef Stalin, Soviet statesman (1879-1953)

Not even mighty warriors can break a frail arrow when it is multiplied and supported by its fellows. As long as you brothers support one another and render assistance to one another, your enemies can never gain the victory over you. But if you fall away from one another, you can be broken like a frail arrow, one at a time.

Genghis Khan, founder of the Mongol empire (1162-1227)

A single arrow is easily broken, but not ten in a bundle.

Japanese proverb

When spiders unite they can tie down a lion.

Ethopian proverb

A paddle here, a paddle there - the canoe stays still.

African proverb

One thing I believe to the fullest is that if you think and achieve as a team, the individual accolades will take care of themselves. Talent wins games, but teamwork and intelligence win championships.

Michael Jordan, US basketball player (b. 1963)

Ask not what your team-mates can do for you. Ask what you can do for your team-mates.

Earvin 'Magic' Johnson, US basketball player (b. 1959)

It's hard to work in groups, when you're omnipotent.

Q, character in 'Star Trek: The Next Generation'

There is no limit to what a man can achieve as long as he doesn't care who gets the credit.

Bob Woodruff, US country singer songwriter

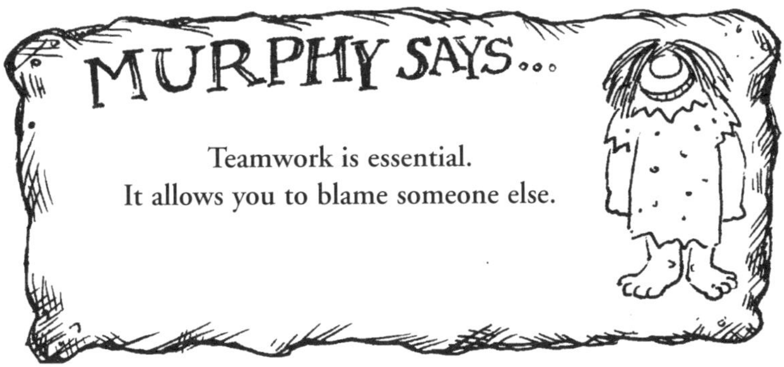

The world is moved along, not only by the mighty shoves of its heroes, but also by the aggregate of the tiny pushes of each honest worker.

Helen Keller, US author, lecturer (1880-1968)

The longer a management team is exposed to the problems of the real world the greater is the need to be prepared for a full range of problems and situations, and to have a team ready to meet them.

Meredith Belbin, US management consultant

TECHNOLOGY

For a list of all the ways technology has failed to improve the quality of life, please press three.

Alice Kahn, US journalist

While modern technology has given people powerful new communication tools, it apparently can do nothing to alter the fact that many people have nothing useful to say.

Lee Gomes, US journalist

Conversations are the way knowledge workers discover what they know, share it with their colleagues, and in the process create new knowledge for the organisation. The panoply of modern information and communication technology - for example, computers, faxes, e-mail - can help knowledge workers in this process. But all depends upon the quality of the conversations that such technologies support.

Alan Webber, US editor, author, business speaker (b. 1948)

Increasing access to technology improves overall wealth, but also exacerbates inequality, because access benefits the information-rich the most.

John Browning, US scientist, author

The most exciting breakthroughs of the 21st century will not occur because of technology but because of an expanding concept of what it means to be human.

John Naisbitt & Patricia Aburdene, US futurist authors

It works better if you plug it in.

Like it or not, we are entering a phase in which the economy is dominated by technology - therefore dominated by increasing returns and by permanent transience instead of equilibrium.

Brian Arthur, Irish economist

THINKING

Few people think more than two or three times a year. I've made an international reputation for myself by thinking once or twice a week.

George Bernard Shaw, Irish playwright, essayist (1856-1950)

The problems that exist in the world today cannot be solved by the level of thinking that created them.

Albert Einstein, German physicist (1879-1955)

Of one thing we can be sure. The quality of our life in the future will be determined by the quality of our thinking.

Edward de Bono, Maltese psychologist, writer (b. 1933)

No one is thinking if everyone is thinking alike.

George S Patton, US general (1885-1945)

Where all think alike, no one thinks very much.

Walter Lippmann, US newspaper commentator, author (1889-1974)

Thought is action in rehearsal.

Sigmund Freud, Austrian founder of psychoanalysis (1856-1939)

Big thinking precedes great achievement.

Wilfred Peterson, US poet, moralist

Ours is a very fast-moving field. You have to be able to step back from it. Many years ago, I decided to take a week every year and absorb myself in thinking many years ahead. I get colleagues to put together what PhD theses I should read, what products I should play with, what memos I should look at. So, it's been, except for sleeping a little bit, day and night all by myself uninterrupted. Now, because things are moving so fast, I do it twice a year.

Bill Gates, US computer engineer, entrepeneur (b. 1955)

If you make people think they're thinking, they'll love you; but if you really make them think, they'll hate you.

Donald Marquis, US newspaper owner, poet, playwright (1878-1937)

All the problems of the world could be settled easily if men were only willing to think. The trouble is that men very often resort to all sorts of devices in order not to think, because thinking is such hard work.

Thomas J Watson, US businessman, founder of IBM (1874-1956)

People demand freedom of speech to make up for the freedom of thought which they avoid.

Soren Kierkegaard, Danish philosopher (1813-1855)

Thinking is the hardest work there is, which is the probable reason why so few engage in it.

Henry Ford, US automobile manufacturer, engineer (1863-1947)

Most people would rather die than think: many do.

Bertrand Russell, British philosopher, mathematician (1872-1970)

Few minds wear out; more rust out.

Christian Nestell Bovee, US author, lawyer (1820-1904)

The brain is a wonderful organ. It starts working when you get up in the morning, and doesn't stop until you get to the office.

Robert Frost, US poet (1874-1963)

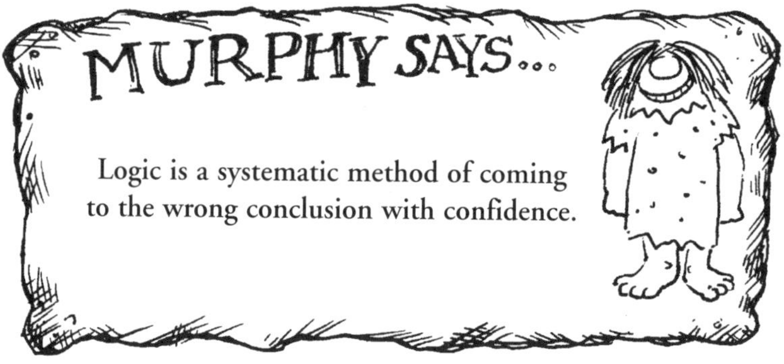

Language shapes the way we think, and determines what we can think about.

Benjamin Whorf, US linguist (1897-1941)

Life does not consist mainly - or even largely - of facts and happenings. It consists mainly of the storm of thoughts that is forever blowing through one's head.

Mark Twain, US author (1835-1910)

All the talk about labour flexibility misses the point. It's not ways of working that need to become more flexible, it's ways of thinking.

Simon Caulkin, British journalist

Far from thinking coming after knowledge, knowledge comes on the coat tails of thinking. Therefore, instead of knowledge-centred schools we need thinking-centred schools. This is no luxury, no Utopian vision of erudite and elitist education. These are hard facts about the way learning works.

David Perkins, US psychologist

TIME

Dost thou love life?
then do not squander time,
for that is the stuff life is made of.

Benjamin Franklin, US statesman, author, scientist (1706-1790)

Write it on your heart that every day is the best day in the year. No man has learned anything rightly, until he knows that every day is Doomsday.

Ralph Waldo Emerson, American essayist, poet (1803-1882)

The only things that start on time are those things that you're late for

He that will not apply new remedies must expect new evils; for time is the greatest innovator.

William Bridges, US engineer, researcher, educator (b. 1934)

We're in such a hurry most of the time we never get much chance to talk. The result is a kind of endless day-to-day shallowness, a monotony that leaves a person wondering years later where all the time went and sorry that it's all gone.

Robert Pirsig, US author (b. 1928)

Time makes more converts than reason.

Thomas Paine, British author, political theorist (1737-1809)

You will never find time for anything. If you want time you must make it.

Charles Buxton, British administrator in South America (1853-1934)

No mind is much employed upon the present. Recollection and anticipation fill up almost all our moments.

Samuel Johnson, British poet, critic, lexicographer (1709-1784)

Until you value yourself, you will not value your time. Until you value your time, you will not do anything with it.

M Scott Peck

The word 'now' is like a bomb through the window, and it ticks.

Arthur Miller, US dramatist (b. 1915)

TRUST

Whether you're on a sports team, in an office or a member of a family, if you can't trust one another, there's going to be trouble.

Joe Paterno, US college football coach (b. 1926)

There's no such thing as 'half-trust'. The instructor pilot can't 'half' sit next to you on your first solo.

Tom Peters, US management author, presenter (b. 1942)

The chief lesson I have learned in a long life is that the only way to make a man trustworthy is to trust him.

Henry Stimson, US statesman (1867-1950)

Set your expectations high; find men and women whose integrity and values you respect; get their agreement on a course of action; and give them your ultimate trust.

John Akers, US business mogul (b. 1934)

Organisational leaders who are motivated by the common good not only reject the role of the dictator who rules by fear; they also recognize that demagogues who seduce followers with false promises cannot maintain the trust essential for cooperation.

Michael Maccoby, US management author, psychologist (b. 1933)

You can buy a person's hand, but you can't buy his heart. You can buy his back but you can't buy his brains.

Stephen Covey, US management author, presenter (b. 1932)

It's been my experience that the people who gain trust, loyalty, excitement and energy fast are the ones who pass on the credit to the people who really have done the work. A leader doesn't need any credit; he's already in the top slot. He's getting more credit than he deserves anyway.

Robert Townsend, US author, businessman (1920-1998)

I don't want any yes-men around me. I want everybody to tell me the truth even if it costs them their jobs.

Samuel Goldwyn, Polish-born US film producer (1882-1974)

When we walk to the edge of all the light we have and take the step into the darkness of the unknown, we must believe that one of two things will happen. There will be something solid for us to stand on or we will be taught to fly.

Patrick Overton

Put not your trust in money, but put your money in trust.

Oliver Wendell Holmes, US essayist, poet (1809-1894)

So, if you have not been trustworthy in handling worldly wealth, who will trust you with true riches?

Luke 16.11

VALUE

What we obtain too cheap we esteem too little; it is dearness only that gives everything its value.

Thomas Paine, British author, political theorist (1737-1809)

Sometimes one pays most for the things one gets for nothing.

Albert Einstein, German physicist (1879-1955)

If you undervalue yourself, no-one's going to come along and raise your price.

David Williams, British management author, presenter (b. 1950)

Steinmetz once charged General Electric $10,000 for chalking an 'X'on a defective machine part. When GE protested and asked him to justify the charge, he sent back this itemised bill - 'Making one chalk mark - $1; Knowing where to place it - $9,999.'

Charles Steinmetz, US electrical engineer (1865-1923)

You don't get paid for the hour. You get paid for the value you bring to an hour.

Jim Rohn, US motivational speaker, author

The individual's most vital need is to prove his worth, and this usually means an insatiable hunger for action. For it is only the few who can acquire a sense of worth by developing and employing their capacities and talents. The majority prove their worth by keeping busy.

Eric Hoffer, US philosopher, author, longshoreman (1902-1983)

VISION

Some things have to be believed to be seen.

Ralph Hodgson, US poet (1871-1962)

Walt Disney died six years before the opening of Walt Disney World. At the opening ceremonies, two Disney executives were sitting together. One said, 'Too bad Walt couldn't have been here to see this.' The other responded, 'You're wrong. Walt did see this, that's why it's here.'

True wisdom consists not in seeing what is immediately before our eyes, but in foreseeing what is to come.

Terence, Roman dramatist (185-129 BC)

Vision is the art of seeing things invisible.

Jonathan Swift, Irish clergyman, poet, satirist (1667-1745)

No man that does not see visions will ever realise any high hope or undertake any high enterprise.

Woodrow Wilson, US President (1856-1924)

A man to carry on a successful business must have imagination. He must see things as in a vision, a dream of the whole thing.

Charles Schwab, US industrialist (1862-1939)

Every man takes the limits of his own field of vision for the limits of the world.

Arthur Schopenhaur, German philosopher (1788-1860)

The most pathetic person in the world is someone who has sight but has no vision.

Helen Keller, US writer, lecturer (1880-1968)

Write the vision and make it plain upon tables, that he may run that readeth it. Where there is no vision the people perish.

Habakkuk 2:2

The entrepreneur is essentially a visualiser and an actualiser. He can visualise something, and when he visualises it he sees exactly how to make it happen.

Robert L Schwartz, US executive, Rolls Royce (b. 1939)

The vision must be followed by the venture. It is not enough to stare up the steps. We must step up the stairs.

Vance Hepner

Vision is the torch of leadership. Shared vision is the spark of great action.

David Williams, British management author, presenter (b. 1950)

One sees great things from the valley, only small things from the peak.

G K Chesterton, British essayist, writer, poet (1874-1936)

The great successful men of the world have used their imaginations, they think ahead and create their mental picture, and then go to work materialising that picture in all its details, filling in here, adding a little there, altering this bit and that bit, but steadily building, steadily building.

Robert Collier, US advertising copywriter

VOICE

The ability to express an idea is well nigh as important as the idea itself.

Bernard Baruch, US statesman, businessman (1870-1965)

The man is only half himself, the other half is his expression.

Ralph Waldo Emerson, American essayist, poet (1803-1882)

A good head and good heart are always a formidable combination. But when you add to that a literate tongue or pen, then you have something very special.

Nelson Mandela, South African statesman (b. 1918)

No leader sets out to be a leader. People set out to live their lives, expressing themselves fully. When that expression is of value they become leaders.

Warren Bennis, US academic, management author (b. 1925)

WINNING

If it doesn't matter who wins, then how come they keep score?

Vince Lombardi, US football coach (1913-1970)

Whoever said, 'It's not whether you win or lose that counts,' probably lost.

Martina Navratilova, Czech-born US tennis player (b. 1956)

The will to win is important, but the will to prepare is vital.

Joe Paterno, US college football coach (b. 1926)

If anything goes bad, I did it. If anything goes semi-good, we did it. If anything goes really good, then you did it. That's all it takes to get people to win football games for you.

Paul 'Bear' Bryant, US football coach (1913-1983)

Desire is one of the immense advantages that the underdog often has: simply wanting to win more than the top dog does.

William Bridges, US engineer, researcher, educator (b. 1934)

He who hesitates is last.

Please don't ask me what the score is, I'm not even sure what the game is.

Ashleigh Brilliant, British philosopher, author (b. 1933)

The trouble with the rat race is that even if you win you're still a rat.

Lily Tomlin, US comic actress (b. 1939)

WISDOM

We can be knowledgeable with other men's knowledge but we cannot be wise with other men's wisdom.

Montaigne, French essayist (1533-1592)

Knowledge is proud that he has learned so much; Wisdom is humble that he knows no more.

William Cowper, British poet (1731-1800)

The older I grow the more I distrust the familiar doctrine that age brings wisdom.

H L Mencken, US journalist (1880-1956)

That which seems the height of absurdity in one generation often becomes the height of wisdom in the next.

John Stuart Mill, British philosopher, economist (1806-1873)

The believer is happy. The doubter is wise.

Hungarian proverb

An optimist is a person who sees a green light everywhere, while a pessimist sees only the red stoplight. The truly wise person is 'colour-blind'.

Albert Schweitzer, Alsatian theologian (1875-1965)

If one is too lazy to think, too vain to do a thing badly, too cowardly to admit it, one will never attain wisdom.

Cyril Connolly, British critic, writer (1903-1974)

Be wiser than other people, if you can, but do not tell them so.

Lord Chesterfield, British diplomat, author (1694-1773)

WORKING

If you don't want to work, you have to work to earn enough money so that you won't have to work.

Ogden Nash, US humorous writer (1902-1971)

Every day I get up and look through the Forbes list of the richest people in America. If I'm not there, I go to work.

Kenich Ohmae, Japanese/US management consultant

The more I want to get something done, the less I call it work.

Richard Bach, US author (b. 1936)

Find out what you like doing best and get someone to pay you for doing it.

Katherine Whitehorn, British journalist (b. 1926)

Work is not man's punishment. It is his reward and his strength and his pleasure.

George Sand, French author (1804-1876)

If you do not feel yourself growing in your work and your life broadening and deepening, if your task is not a perpetual tonic to you, you have not found your place.

Orison Swett Marden, US editor, author (1850-1924)

Being busy does not always mean real work. The object of all work is production or accomplishment and to either of these ends there must be forethought, system, planning, intelligence, and honest purpose, as well as perspiration. Seeming to do is not doing.

Thomas Alva Edison, US inventor (1847-1931)

My grandfather once told me that there were two kinds of people: those who do the work and those who take the credit. He told me to try to be in the first group; there was much less competition.

Indira Gandhi, Indian Prime Minister (1917-1984)

Good work is always done in defiance of management.

Robert Woodward, US journalist

It's not enough to be busy. The question is, what are we busy about?

Henry David Thoreau, US essayist, poet (1817-1862)

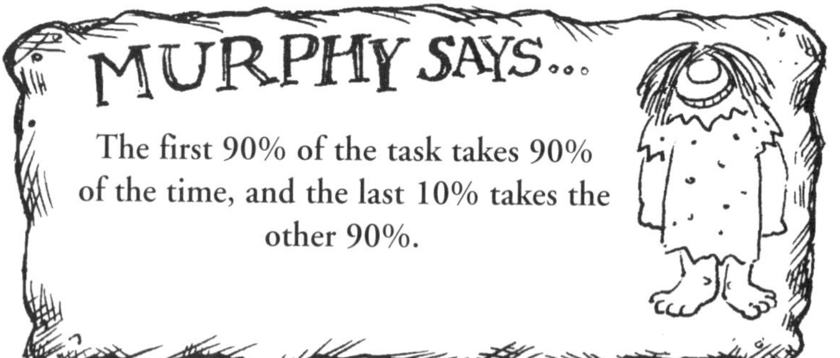

No race can prosper till it learns there is as much dignity in tilling a field as in writing a poem.

Booker T Washington, US educator (1856-1915)

By working faithfully 8 hours a day you may eventually get to be a boss and work 12 hours a day.

Robert Frost, US poet (1874-1963)

A man who works with his hands is a labourer; a man who works with his hands and his brain is a craftsman; but a man who works with his hands and his brain and his heart is an artist.

Louis Nizer, British lawyer (1902-1994)

There is no easy method of learning difficult things. The method is to close the door, give out that you are not at home, and work.

Joseph Marie De Maistre, French diplomat, writer (1753-1821)

In order that people may be happy in their work, these three things are needed: they must be fit for it; they must not do too much of it; and they must have a sense of success in it.

John Ruskin, British writer, art critic (1819-1900)

The superstition that all our hours of work are a minus quantity in the happiness of life, and all the hours of idleness are plus ones, is a most ludicrous and pernicious doctrine, and its greatest support comes from our not taking sufficient trouble, not making a real effort, to make work as near pleasure as it can be.

Lord Balfour, British Prime Minister (1848-1930)

The law of work does seem utterly unfair - but there it is, and nothing can change it; the higher the pay in enjoyment the worker gets out of it, the higher shall be his pay in money also.

Mark Twain, US author (1835-1910)

Work seven days a week and nothing can stop you.

John Moores, British entrepreneur, philanthropist (1896-1993)

The Encyclopedia of Famous Last Words does not contain the entry 'I wish I'd spent more time at the office.'